Hiking Without Dave

A journey of things found, lost, and remembered along Ohio's Buckeye Trail

CW Spencer

Copyright © 2014 CW Spencer
All rights reserved.
No part of this book may be stored, reproduced, or transmitted in any form or by any means without prior written permission of the author. The only exception is brief quotations in printed reviews.

All events in this book are true. Any mistakes as to content are in no way intentional; they are products of the author's own recollection and interpretation of his experiences. No names have been changed to protect the innocent, but last names have mercifully been omitted.

ISBN-13: 978-0-9907502-0-8

Cover design by Michael L. Smith
Cover photo © 2014 Bonnie Spencer
Interior photos are the property of CW Spencer
and are used with permission from the subjects.
Journal maps were designed by CW and Bonnie Spencer
and are not drawn to scale.
The Buckeye Trail map is used with permission from the
Buckeye Trail Association.

Published by Lamp·Light Publishing

Thy word is a lamp unto my feet, and a light unto my path.
~ Psalm 119:105 (KJV)

Printed in the United States of America

To Dave
You left us way too early

To all those souls experiencing the loss
of a loved one to suicide

CONTENTS

Preface	vii
Note to Reader	ix
Introduction: Dear Dave	1
PART ONE: Remembering Innocent Times	5
Journal Entry #1: Remembering the Important Stuff	7
Journal Entry #2: Finding the Inner Child Together	15
Journal Entry #3: Finding Friends in High and Low Places	21
Journal Entry #4: Losing My Cool	27
Journal Entry #5: Finding a Way to Get Over It	33
Journal Entry #6: Finding a Trail Name	41
Journal Entry #7: Finding Shelter	49
Journal Entry #8: Finding the Shepherd	57
Journal Entry #9: Finding a Good Book	63
Journal Entry #10: Losing Brain Cells	67
Journal Entry #11: Finding Kindred Spirits	77
Journal Entry #12: Finding Cover	85
Journal Entry #13: Finding Nourishment for Body and Soul	93

PART TWO: Losing Direction — 99

   Journal Entry #14: Remembering Some Valleys — 101

   Journal Entry #15: Finding Common Ground — 107

   Journal Entry #16: Finding the Message — 113

   Journal Entry #17: Losing Traction — 119

   Journal Entry #18: Losing the Battle — 129

   Journal Entry #19: Finding My Role — 137

   Journal Entry #20: Losing the Way — 145

   Journal Entry #21: Finding False Assurance — 153

PART THREE: Finding Hope and Healing — 159

   Journal Entry #22: Finding Unexpected Blessings — 161

   Journal Entry #23: Finding Clues — 171

   Journal Entry #24: Remembering the Big Picture — 177

   Journal Entry #25: Remembering the Good Ole Days — 183

   Journal Entry #26: Remembering a Son — 191

   Final Journal Entry — 201

Afterword — 203

Acknowledgments — 205

Notes — 209

Buckeye Trail Map — 211

PREFACE

This is not a hiking guide.

Though I did hike the entire length of the Buckeye Trail, it was not my intention to write meticulous travel instructions. For one thing, I'm not fond of doing research. For another, Robert J. Pond has written an excellent resource: *Follow the Blue Blazes*.

Nor did I want to do a day-by-day, mile-by-mile story of my travels. John N. Merrill already has a detailed account of his 60-day trip on the then 1,310-mile trail around Ohio. Since I don't do details well, this would not have been a good strategy for me. Even if I do happen to take notes, they have a habit of disappearing, only to reappear far in the future when they are no longer of any use.

I have, however, attempted to convey some of the sights and sounds that captured my attention on the trail. I want you to walk with the people I walked with and experience the beauty, difficulties, and totally unexpected adventures I found along the way.

More importantly, though, I want to share some new insights I gained and some old memories that resurfaced that I hope will touch your life in a positive way. My wish is to inform, entertain, and inspire you. My experience proved to me that good can come from an impossibly bad situation—even from the suicide of a loved one. My story is not meant to be heavy, just real.

This is really my best effort to explain how I feel about my kid brother Dave.

CW Spencer—2014

NOTE TO READER

Hiking Without Dave is two stories woven into one. One story tells of the adventures I had while hiking the Buckeye Trail. It is written as a journal to my brother, my way of sharing my journey with him. The second story is about another journey—the one my brother and I lived together over the 47 years of his life. Each chapter of the book begins with a journal entry that relates some of my experiences on one of the twenty-six sections of the trail. Each journal entry is followed by a personal memory I have of Dave.

I did not hike the trail sections in order. Like some of my friends, I hiked whenever and wherever I found someone else who needed to hike the same miles, so you will find that the journal sections of the book do not follow the Buckeye Trail in order. Also, they are not entirely in the order I hiked them. Liberty was taken in arranging them for the flow of the story. Nonetheless, the first journal entry describes my first hike, and the journal ends with the steps that completed my travels. For those of you who like to keep the big picture in mind, a map of the entire Buckeye Trail can be found at the end of the book.

Dear Dave

I'm thinking about us again. That's something that happens almost every day. Even though my mind goes back far too many times to that Memorial Day weekend, I have good memories as well. I try to linger on those as often as possible. They inevitably include our trips, whether by boat, bikes, or boots. Seems like our best way to connect was to share time together outdoors.

I can hear those waves slapping our rowboat, anchored in our sweet spot in the bay at Rice Lake. The rest of the family might have chosen to loaf at the cabin or drive into Peterborough, but *we* were there to fish. From our metal perches, we pulled out endless bass and walleyes. And don't forget that one illegal species you kept. I haven't.

I can see the newly emerged greens and smell the woodsy aromas that we encountered as we pedaled down the Greenbrier River Trail in West Virginia on a spring morning. Fifty miles on my little Huffy is hard to forget. Why did it always turn into a race to see who would get to that little diner in Marlinton first?

I can feel the vastness of the Red River Gorge that we experienced as we explored its boundless natural beauty. Kentucky certainly has bragging rights over your state (in my not-so-humble opinion). We joked endlessly about each other's state. In fact, we joked about almost everything. I appreciated the humor, especially since we didn't do conflict well. Except for our love of the outdoors—and for each other—we didn't have a lot in common. Our differences were nearly as immense as the gorge, and sometimes being together took some work. But we did the work and didn't let it stop us from having fun.

Maybe my best memories are of the times we met halfway—in more ways than one—deep in southern Ohio at the Day Hike Trail at Shawnee State Park. Previous to that, we had drifted apart, so I was excited when, by some stroke of fate, or more likely of a Divine hand, we decided to drive a few hours to join forces in conquering some rugged terrain. Those steep hills of the "Little Smokies" soon became our regular spot, and that's where, on one frosty winter afternoon, we came up with The Plan.

The Appalachian Trail beckoned us to a thru-hike. None of those puny three- or four-day hikes we had taken before. Can you imagine if we would have actually gotten to carry out our plan? Who would have survived the longest on Ramen noodles and Doritos? Would we have escaped the clutches of the many bears that lurked along the path? Whose stinky boots would have rendered the other brother unconscious first?

It wasn't malnutrition, beasts, or body odors, however, that stopped us before we even made it to Mount Springer. Those things we could have overcome. Now I'll never know how our big hike would have turned out. This is where the bad memories return, and no amount of humor can chase them away.

I still need to hike—for us—but the AT is a bigger project than I want to handle alone. I remember a short backpacking trip I made years ago on Ohio's Buckeye Trail, the largest hiking loop anyone knows of. More to me than just a 1,444-mile trail along back roads and through forests and cities, the BT winds a path through my life. Its southern terminus is just across the river at the overlook in Eden Park, the view we shared when you came to visit.

It winds its way near the Day Hike Trail that you and I loved so much. It passes through hills that I explored as a child in northeastern Ohio (you were still a rug rat at the time). Finally, it leads past a plot of ground in Troy where rests a part of me. This could be the perfect answer.

As I prepare to step off, many feelings are coursing through me: anxiety about what I will encounter, excitement for a new adventure, loneliness that you will not be walking with me, fear of not finding the answers I'm looking for. I know it won't be easy, but I also know that this is the way for me to go.

Since I can't hike the AT with you, I'll take this circular route with your memory. I need to clear my head and air out my heart. I've told family and friends I'm still going on a big hike, just that on this adventure I'll be hiking without Dave.

Part One

Remembering Innocent Times

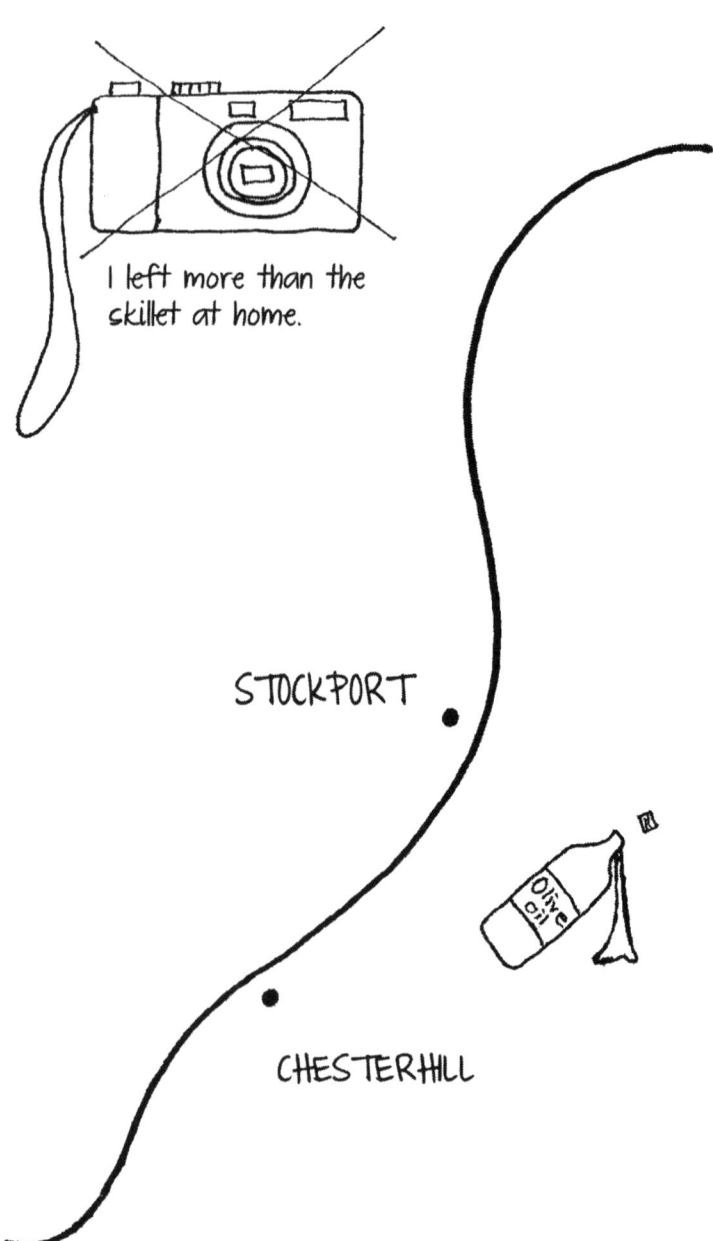

Journal Entry # 1

Remembering the Important Stuff

I decided to go big on my kick-off hike, Dave. Along with eleven others, I would hike through a large piece of the Stockport section and cross well into the next.

It had taken me a week or two to decide on this trip featured on the Buckeye Trail website. When I finally called John, the organizer of the hike, he said I was lucky I didn't wait any longer. There were twelve slots, and I was number twelve. He advised me that the terrain was strenuous and to pack accordingly.

With no Dairy Queens, Bob Evanses, Pizza Huts, or Cracker Barrels on the trail, I had to go prepared. For a good part of a week, I stuffed and unstuffed and restuffed items (each one absolutely indispensable) into and out of and back into my pack, which was newly acquired from my official outfitter: Sam's Club. I bought one exactly like the one I gave you. It sure is a beauty.

I heard there were bears in southern Ohio. I kinda hoped to see one, but then what? It's hard to scurry with forty-plus pounds in tow, much of the tonnage being classic bear cuisine. I had already shaved some weight by leaving the cast iron skillet, bacon, eggs, and potatoes at home.

That pan really went over big on the AT when the thru-hikers got wind of it, didn't it? Even though those guys ribbed us about it, they had to admit that we cooked up the best breakfast on the trail. You and I were our own kind of cool, and that is one of the reasons I liked doing stuff with you.

As prepared as I thought I was for this hike, I found out quickly that I was the only member of the group without a camera. Logically, I was the one elected to point-and-shoot for each person's group shot. Somehow I still managed to get into the photo that found its way into the BT newsletter. Even in black and white, I thought I looked a little green.

It was time for me to look the hiker, so I dropped some cool terms you and I had picked up from our few weeks on the AT. Terms like "ultralight hiking," "cotton is evil," and "slackpacking." I couldn't see anyone's eyes behind their hiking shades, but I was sure they had to be wide open in amazement.

We headed south from Stockport, hiking up and down and around the hills. That part of Ohio reminds me of your West Virginia. Farms are carved out of the woodlands, spread about as thinly as the hairs on my bald spot. It seemed like we ascended most of the time. I was glad I took a ton of food because my heavy pack gave me a fierce appetite.

I kept getting a whiff of olives, but it didn't quite match the scent coming from the prolific autumn-olive trees covering the hills. I found the source when we reached our camp and I peered into my pack. The lid had popped off my pint of cold-pressed extra virgin olive oil, and everything in my food bag was soaked. The good news? All my food had become considerably healthier.

I felt people watching as I dumped out the precious extract. Some oil had also leaked into my pack. As I generated the appropriate surprised looks and sounds to make this type of event seem unbelievably rare, I was relieved to see heads begin to turn away from me. My short-lived relief changed to alarm when I saw a zombie stagger into camp.

Well, actually the zombie was a hiker named Bob. He dropped his monstrous pack, then pulled a chair out of it and plopped down. As he slowly changed back to human, he told us his story.

His transformation from man to monster had started earlier that day. He had been late for our departure, so he spent the day playing catch-up. The heat and humidity were oppressive for late April, and it didn't help that he had fifty pounds or more (just a guess) on his back. All of this caused him to become exhausted, then disoriented. No one in the group knew he was behind us. Although he was only a couple of miles from camp, it might as well have been a hundred since there was no cell service.

Out of nowhere, a car had pulled up beside him on the dead-end dirt road he was on. When he managed to bring the driver's face into focus, he slowly began to realize help had arrived. The "angel" who found Bob told him he had no idea what had made him turn down that path-of-a-road. Bob, however, said that *he* knew why: God had sent him.

As I watched our new arrival wobble on that chair, I wondered what business he had hiking. As he watched oil drip out of my bag, he probably wasn't so sure about me either. I'm sure you would think he and I would make the ultimate BT hiking team.

The next day was even tougher. Bob again struggled, so the two of us went at a slower pace than the rest of the group. We stopped for breakfast at a diner in the village of Chesterhill. In the afternoon, we rested by a creek and I made some tea for us. He couldn't figure out what was wrong. He was a fit and experienced hiker, having already completed a considerable portion of the Buckeye Trail.

We finally realized we were not going to make it to camp. Luckily, this part of the trail was on a back road and a second trail angel came to the rescue. Bob had recovered enough to walk, so he and I hiked together to camp while Jay hauled our packs in his truck. Slackpacking was definitely my hiker word for that day.

On day three Bob went home. He found out a few days later that he had pneumonia; the doc told him it was a miracle he had made it as far as he did.

At the end of the fourth day, I was thinking of dropping out myself. After twelve really tough miles and a treacherous, muddy ascent into camp, I was spent. I was looking for sympathy from someone. Anyone. That's when Pat said, "Don't get down on us, CW." *Not* what I was wanting to hear. However, I later realized those were the exact words I *needed* to hear.

For me, this hike is about manning up. If I can handle the physical part, maybe I will find the courage to deal with the intense sadness and toxic guilt I feel. Maybe I can discover what you were thinking, inviting me to spend that last weekend with you, and why you did what you did to me.

Those words from Pat were enough to jolt me into the manly me. These guys are real men. You would have liked them, starting on that first night as they held off laughing until I had most of the oil cleaned out of my bag. Our kind of people. I noticed that Pat hugged everyone good-bye after the hike. Real men do hug.

I survived the entire 56 miles, and I know I want to keep hiking the trail—that is, as soon as the oozing poison ivy dries up and the patches of marble-sized blisters on my feet recede. I have made new friends, and I have an expanded list and some new definitions of hiker words that you would like:

- Cotton is evil—If your sock is made of it, and it gets wet, it will corrupt your sole.
- Ultralight hiking—Probably more involved than losing the skillet.

- Slackpacking—Ultra-ultralight hiking.
- Trail magic—Hot pizza that Jay brought in.
- Leave no trace—Eating all the pizza.
- Hiker trash—A pile of empty pizza boxes.
- Gearhead—Somebody who would have brought calamine lotion, tape, moleskin, and ibuprofen.
- Power hiker—Me going downhill towards camp.
- Cowboy camping—Staying a night or two at the Best Western next time.
- Trail Angels—Those who pick us up and put us back on the trail, and those who help to keep us on it.

As green as I was, it was probably best that my first hiking adventure on the BT was photo-free. However, when I go back to finish the Stockport section, I will make sure I pack my camera.

ONE DAY I TOLD DAD how much I wished he could experience Dave's and my exciting adventures. His response was to give me his camera and tell me to go take some pictures for him. This happened just in time for our trip along the Cranberry River in West Virginia.

Dave said it would be a good workout if we rode our bikes up the service road along the river. I agreed to that since we were always looking for ways to burn calories. As we conquered the mountain, we traded the camera back and forth, snapping each other while we sucked in our guts. We would need to come up with something better than that, though, to impress Dad.

Dave wanted me to get in a good shot or two of his bike, which cost sixteen times as much as mine (and I bought mine new).

Then he asked, "Hey Squooge, how about a side shot of your Huffy?"

"Okay, but don't get any ideas. You can't have it."

"Probably a wise idea. I don't think I could handle the torque those gears put out."

After quite a few miles of torquing uphill on the gravel road, I was glad to see it level off and then turn into a downhill stretch. But neither of us was prepared for what lay ahead.

A bear the size of a pickup truck was parked at the bottom right in the middle of the bend. Dust rose as we jammed on the brakes. It was then that Dave chose to tell me that "bad bears" were shipped to this preserve. People knew that and went through at their own risk. I bet most people find this out *before* they see one—and better yet, before *it* sees *them*. I secretly wished that I had Dave's bike instead of mine.

Suddenly, Dave remembered the camera. A real bear! A bad bear! This would be the photo to impress Dad. With trembling hands we snapped five or six pictures, trying to position the camera to create the illusion of us petting the bear. After all, even bad bears need love.

After ten long minutes, the bear sauntered off into the woods. I guess it figured it would go stir up trouble somewhere else. We gave it ten more minutes, then raced down the hill. Halfway down, I yelled, "What if her cub shows up when we go past?" Dust rose again as we locked up our brakes and sent gravel flying. Then we realized simultaneously that stopping near the bottom wouldn't help our cause, so we gassed it again. We skidded around the turn and pedaled frantically until at least one bad bear would no longer be a threat.

What a trip! We had already fondly named our bear Kong. And we had proof of our bravery for once.

When I got home, I immediately retrieved Dad's camera from my backpack. Almost as excited as a hungry bear in a freshly-stocked trout stream, I prepared to remove the film. My hands trembled again, but this time in anticipation of what would come back from the developer. I would have to handle the film with kid gloves. Dad would soon be able to see firsthand that all the bragging Dave and I did was true. I opened the camera carefully to avoid any light exposure to its contents.

I needn't have bothered—I stared into an empty cavity.

I spent the next few hours deciding what sort of prevarication I would use on Dave when he asked where the pictures were. Finally, though, the spiritual side of me kicked in and I began to ponder: What would Jesus do?

That didn't help. He probably would have made sure film was in the camera.

Eventually I fessed up, giving Dave so much ammo for future jokes that he would likely need a background check. Come to think of it, though, he fired very few shots concerning the empty camera. I hope I would have shown the same restraint if the tables had been turned. It was quite a while before I told Dad, and then I did only because he was relentless in asking to see the pictures.

At some point I finally stopped lamenting that I had not captured my Kodak moment. After all, what's more important—a photograph or the adventure itself? Without photographic proof, I can make our Cranberry trip, including the bear, as big and as bad as I want it to be. Sometimes the best pictures for me are the ones developed only in my mind.

BELLE VALLEY SECTION

RED HILL FARM

BELLE VALLEY

CALDWELL

"Jaws" at Red Hill Farm

Journal Entry #2

Finding the Inner Child Together

When Zombie Bob and Olive Oil Man first met, I had a sneaking feeling that we would knock off more miles together. Sometimes you just know. After the spectacles we made of ourselves on the Stockport hike, I figured we deserved each other. Well, we teamed up again for my second hike. I'm glad we did because I'm enjoying hiking with Bob.

This one was not as ambitious as my first hike. We returned to the same general area for only one day in the Belle Valley section. When we passed through the gate and into the pastures of Red Hill Farm, we were surprised to encounter a huge gorilla and a giant land shark. Fortunately, we managed to "shoot" them both and get out alive. We hadn't known how dangerous the Belle Valley section could be.

I didn't find out about the monstrous bear that resides at the farm until a week later when I called the owners to thank them for giving a right-of-way to the Buckeye Trail. Otherwise, I would have shot a picture of it as well since I had both camera *and* film this hike. (I'm sure you remember our Cranberry trip when we met Kong. I still grimace when I recall opening up Dad's camera afterward.)

OK, so the creatures were stone monoliths, and I was just playing. The BT is bringing out the kid in your sometimes-too-serious older brother.

One thing you and I missed was being kids together. By the time you were promoted to third grade, I was off to college. I wonder what it was like for you. Did Dad sing "Ole Shep" and tuck you into bed? Did the two of you play a lot of catch? Did Mom spoil you, too? Did she warn you about the boogeyman before you set out trick-or-treating?

Speaking of the boogeyman, I think he almost caught up with Bob and me when we returned months later to finish hiking this section. It wasn't even Halloween. It was early January, in weather I would have previously thought too cold for man or monster.

We had organized a three-day, 45-mile hike, planning to camp nightly like true cowboys at the Best Western. Our hike began normally enough. After a while, though, we realized we would need something to supplement our hiker food on that rugged terrain. At the end of the first day of hiking, although it was a decent drive, we were blessed to discover Caldwell Pizza Factory, and the next day rediscover it, and the next day... We didn't starve on this trip, that was for sure.

We averaged fifteen miles per day, not bad on those Appalachian foothills, trying to burn off the carbs. The trail followed pleasant back roads, picturesque reclaimed strip mining land, and stretches of woods.

The directions for the second day's leg should have raised a huge red flag in our pizza-addled brains: "The BT begins a meander that leads generally SW along a ridge on a variety of bull-dozed trails. Watch carefully for blazes!" We faded into the trees at about half past three on that frosty afternoon.

It became clear after a while that we were not exactly proficient at meandering. In fact, it began to look as if we were going to get caught by the early January night with no apparent exit from the haunted forest. We needed to find one of those blue blazes that mark the Buckeye Trail, the sooner the better since our lights, matches, and tents were back in the car.

I couldn't remember what Mom said the boogeyman would do to me besides steal my candy. I'm sure she never told me how I could identify him or if he had any special powers to guard against. At that moment, though, I figured he could smell fear (and probably pizza breath), so I tried to ignore the noises under the trees and concentrate on breathing through my nose. Thinking positive thoughts was in the plan as well. *We are two grown men, Bob's a Boy Scout leader, and we aren't scared.* But I think Bob and I, like the boogeyman, could smell a little fear in each other. As I look back on it, getting scared like little kids was one of the best parts of the hike.

Then it happened. No, silly, not the boogeyman, but we saw a blue blaze. In twenty-five minutes we were in the car. I guess he'll just have to wait a bit longer to collect. Maybe heeding Mom's warning was all it took for me to evade him.

A NEW SEA MONSTER ate up the entire screen at the drive-in theater, more paralyzing and fearsome than any ten land-bound creatures (including black bears). "It's only a movie," Dave and I kept assuring each other. The 85-foot-long eating machine on the other side of the windshield was really only a 15-foot animatron with rubber skin in a studio. More importantly, Jaws required salt water with his dinner, so we hoped the chance of encountering him in the Cumberland River was less than catching a glimpse of the boogeyman.

We loved the primitive campground at Cave Creek, south of Burnside, Kentucky. When we camped there, a trip to the drive-in north of Burnside on Route 27 was always on the schedule. So was a moonlight swim.

It was always a thrill to jump from the cliffs. We tingled at the thought of leaping into the unknown, especially on this eerie, moonless night. No chance we would hit the bottom after our dark descent delivered us into the swiftly moving water—we had tested the depth of the river many times before—but every chance we would become objects of culinary interest to catfish, snapping turtles, and tonight, straight from the big screen . . .

We took the plunge, then swam out to deeper water, trying to forget the carnage we had witnessed in the movie just hours before. Still fresh in our minds were the Ginsu-knife teeth and gallons of blood, the sound of bones being crunched like tortilla chips, and the screams that echoed in the darkness. We tried not to think about the submarine-sized leviathan that could be mere yards behind us sizing us up for his entrée.

We finally came to our senses. One adult, one teen, on our last night at camp. Let's just enjoy the swim. Until Dave began singing: "duh-duh, Duh-Duh, DUH-DUH!"

Panic seized us both and the race to the shore began. It was so dark that I figured we would crash into the rocks at the river's edge before we saw them. At least it might have knocked us unconscious before the chewing started.

To our great relief, though, we escaped the water without major incident. As we dried off, the clouds briefly parted—just long enough for moonlight to fall on the faint outline of a dorsal fin, smoothly circling in the exact spot Dave and I had minutes before so hastily exited.

I wasn't sure I had actually seen it, so I asked Dave. He quickly confirmed the sighting. Had we not made it out of the water, we would have been in serious trouble, no rifle or oxygen tank between the two of us out there.

Back at camp, we laughed at the silliness of our fears, not being able to recall one sighting (besides our manufactured one) of a great white in the Cumberland River, at least not in modern history. I stretched out on my cot, weary from the day's adventures.

Before long, from the other side of the tent, came the haunting refrain: "duh-duh, Duh-Duh, DUH-DUH!" Thank goodness I was not out on the water! But I was positive something had just moved under my cot.

Although Dave and I had not been kids in the same decade, that day we were children together.

SCIOTO TRAIL SECTION

Bob, Jerry, and Karen

TAR HOLLOW
STATE PARK

SCIOTO TRAIL
STATE PARK

PIKE LAKE
STATE PARK

US 23

Journal Entry #3

Finding Friends in High and Low Places

I know you thought that I spent too much time being a diplomat, but you do have to admit that I'm pretty good at it. I've been practicing since I was a kid. I thought my skills might come in handy on a day in late May when Bob and I (yep, back together again) approached three horseback riders who rested their mounts high on a ridge in the Scioto Trail section.

We were weary from a morning of sloshing through the muck of the horse trail. During the dry season, there is no mud to complicate walking on those paths; also, horses that navigate neglected trails tend to keep them open for hikers. However, we weren't thinking about those positives as the slimy mix oozed up and over our boots that day.

You know I have trouble speaking up. Bob, however, is quite often inclined to speak his mind. That's not necessarily a bad thing. Nevertheless, it's usually better to "battle" on your own turf. The folks on the ridge seemed right at home there.

When we approached the riders, Bob spoke first. "Thanks a lot for my muddy boots and socks."

Good one, Bob.

"You're welcome. Most hikers are not as polite as you are."

Zing.

Okay. Time for me to enter the conversation. I brought out one of my specialties: I changed the subject.

"Sure is a hot one."

Fortunately, we all agreed on the weather report. Gradually the meeting became friendlier and more relaxed as the conversation was redirected to more pleasant topics. It was great to feel biases dissolve and to want to share the trail with people who travel by a different mode. However, what got to me the most was that the riders offered to pose for a picture when it was time to travel on. To me, this said that all was well, and I always like to part that way when possible. Bob and I will probably not complain again about horses on the trail—at least not until the next time our shoes are buried in it.

I call this section of the trail "AT Lite," and I know you would've loved it. It winds through three state forests, with camping available at the state parks. Bob and I placed cars at both ends of each day's route. When we finished hiking for the day, we rounded them up and drove to a place to sleep. Since there were no Best Westerns handy, we drove to one of the parks each night and hunkered down in "Old Dodge": Bob in his Journey and me in my Caravan.

The second morning, after shuttling the cars into the proper positions, we hit the trail again. It wasn't long before we met up with Karen and Jerry down in a valley along Route 23. I was amazed to learn that they had started a hike in February on the East Coast. They were following the American Discovery Trail back towards their home in California. The ADT connects with the BT in Chesterhill, Ohio, then piggybacks it for more than 400 miles until it goes its own way at Eden Park in Cincinnati.

Talking above the noise of the heavy traffic on 23, we questioned those hiking heroes. They carried their life on their backs, hiked ten miles a day despite blisters, bugs, and blizzards, and willingly abandoned family, friends, home, and vehicles in order to make their journey together. On a few occasions, they even had to stealth camp in the woods or fields along the road.

I had heard about this type of camping before. When darkness starts to settle in, hikers find a spot to go off the road or path and set up a fireless, no-frills camp. When the sun comes up, they quickly pack up and get going again. Karen and Jerry did this only when necessary.

In the three months they had been on the trail, camping under the radar had only failed once, and failed badly. They had been looking for a spot as daylight was just beginning to fade. Some folks working in their yard suggested a field about a quarter of a mile down the road. When Karen and Jerry found the field, they quickly pitched their tent, fixed a little supper, and stretched their weary bodies out on their sleeping pads. But just as they started to drift off into dreamland, they were abruptly awakened by the property owner yelling and pounding on the tent. He sent them packing, and I'll have to ask them someday what they did that night after they left the forbidden field.

They expressed interest in our hike, but I felt a little embarrassed as I explained my method. My plan is to hike two or three days at a time, rough it only when necessary (or when I forget some equipment), and probably cancel for bad weather. It sounded puny after hearing of their exploits. However, they thought our system was great, so who am I to say different.

Since we were hiking in opposite directions, we had to part, but we are looking forward to meeting again in a few weeks when they reach the Cincinnati area. They will be close enough to my house that, for at least one night, they won't have to pitch their tent or light their stoves.

24   Hiking Without Dave

When the day ended, Bob and I headed home. I thought about the new friends I had acquired over the last couple of days. I don't care what people say about Californians; anyone with guts enough to sneak into the woods to sleep is all right in my book. I don't care what they say about horse people. Those folks weren't so bad, either. I'll just have to remember to lace my boots up tighter and watch where I step the next time I am on a horse trail.

I'm coming to the realization that the stereotypes I have of various groups of people are meaningless. The real people are the ones I connect with each day, one person at a time.

That even goes for folks in West Virginia.

I DON'T REMEMBER EXACTLY WHEN we began swapping West Virginia-Kentucky jokes, but it may have been when Dave purchased his first home. It was situated on a narrow ledge on the side of a mountain. I kidded him about his small slanting yard: anything round or with wheels had to be secured or it would have gone over the edge. We hiked up and down the side of that mountain when I visited because I was worried that if I stood around too long in one place, I might have to shop for pants with two different leg-lengths. Nevertheless, the house was Dave's and he was happy. He and Betty made sure that I had every comfort when I stayed.

He must have lost one too many circular objects, though, because he eventually bought a home down in a lower section of Wayne County, one with a spacious, and basically flat, back yard. The property was graced by a dozen or so large trees and bordered by a wide stream.

Dave loved to sit on the back deck, perched in his recliner (I asked if the fridge would come out next) with a huge mug of steaming coffee and a work by Hemingway, or perhaps Homer, as he watched the beautiful stream flow by. It was another day to contemplate the mower sitting quietly in the middle of the yard. One side of the lawn was mowed (not freshly), the other side not yet. Maybe today would be the day. Maybe not. Manicured grass wasn't at the top of Dave's agenda. I think the rabbits and killdeer in the grass knew and appreciated that today would probably not be the day. The score for the season so far stood at Lazy Boy, 43; Lawn Boy, ½.

It was not because Dave was lazy; it was because he savored the time that he was not installing or repairing computers. He needed the downtime, and he wasn't going to mow the grass just because the neighbors mowed—or didn't mow—theirs.

Customers and friends came to his yard to partake of his technical savvy (his office was in his house) or to be entertained by his quick wit. Dave kept folks on their toes. He could be a fun-loving agitator, much like Dad, or a sensitive, gentle spirit like Mom. He was a blend of intellectual and down-home, and was well-liked by everyone. The driveway could hold Escalades from the city or giant trucks from up in the "fur hills," a car owned by a senator or one owned by a city laborer, and whenever possible, a Caravan belonging to his brother from Kentucky.

LOVELAND SECTION

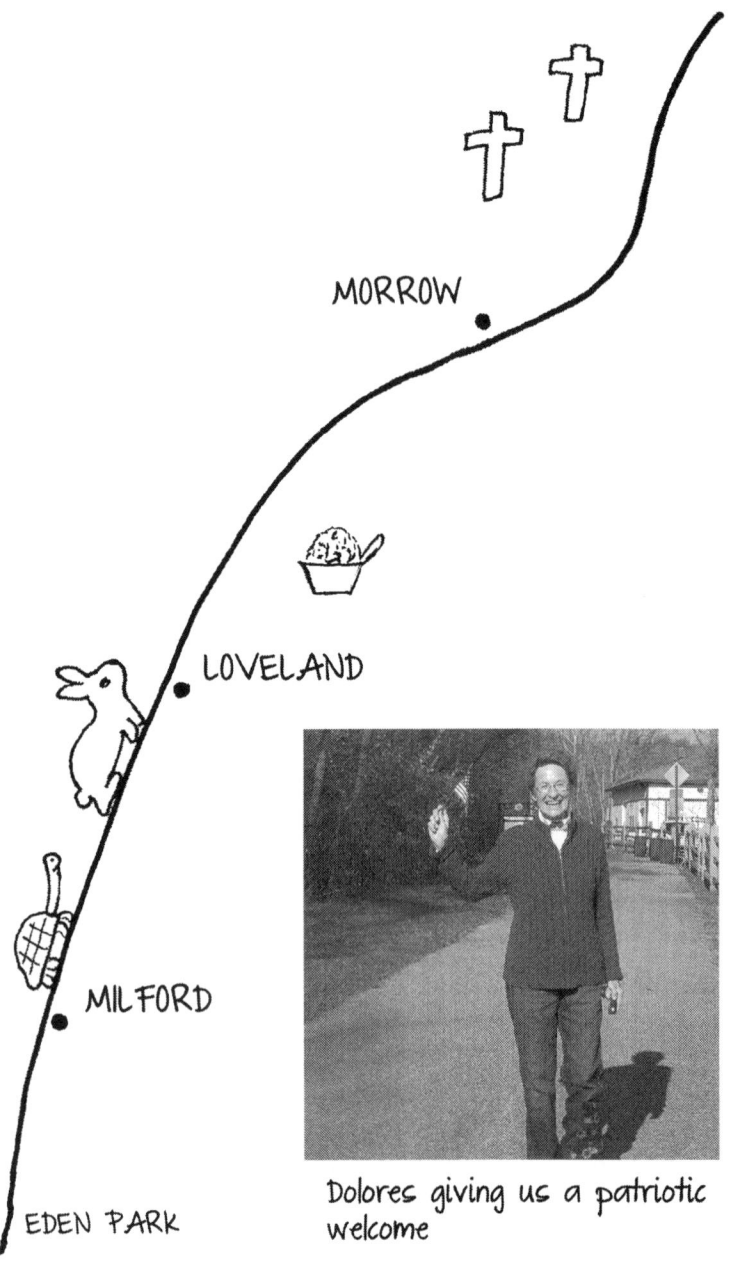

Dolores giving us a patriotic welcome

Journal Entry #4

Losing My Cool

It was already getting hot when Bonnie and I left Milford on a July morning. This was the first of four separate trips I would make to complete the Loveland section. We were bound and determined to reach Loveland—me sometime that day, Bonnie by noon.
- She likes to get physical exercise over with.
- She likes to check it off her list.
- She likes to reap the reward. (That day it happened to be a pina colada flavored Hawaiian shave ice.)

I almost thought I heard her peel out when we started. I realized I would be doing a lot of catch-up that day, but I didn't care. I was just glad that she was hiking with me, though maybe I should have rented some roller blades.

The Buckeye Trail joins the Little Miami Scenic Trail south of Milford and follows it to the northern end of the Loveland section. The LMST is part of the Little Miami State Park. The park is unusual because it is approximately 50 miles long but averages only 66 feet wide. From end to end, a trail is paved along the former Little Miami Railroad. No motorized vehicles are permitted. That was too bad for me that day.

We appreciated the "Bike on your left!" proclamations that kept us from getting run over. A bicycle-built-for-two gave me an idea for keeping up with Bonnie in the future. The variety of bikes that passed us that day reminded me of those you and I saw on our rides in the parks and on the forest trails of West Virginia. You were always on your high-end machine; I tagged along on my $50 Huffy. No one makes fun of, or even notices, my Huffy anymore. I really miss that.

As I lagged behind, I contemplated the old fable *The Tortoise and the Hare*. I was always partial to the plodder; he was pokey, but he didn't let anything stop him from reaching his destination.

Imagine my surprise when the main characters made an appearance. First on stage was the tortoise, the size of a dinner plate, attempting to cross the pavement. Bonnie stopped long enough to poke a stick at it and for me to catch up. We took off again.

Before long we spotted the hare waiting to make its entrance from the grassy shoulder. It was a bit more successful in keeping Bonnie's attention. Obviously a kindred spirit, she was able to get surprisingly close to the bunny before it hopped away. She raced off as well, both of them determined to stay ahead of the tortoises.

Bonnie would soon be able to check this hike off her list. It looked as if she might even make her noon deadline, which would get her a gold star as well.

I was burning up, not only from the heat of the day, but also from working so hard to keep up. I could almost hear the Hawaiian Ice calling my name. Even with my Dr. Scholl's (that you always made fun of), I couldn't beat her that day. I guess she didn't know how the fable ends.

The next day we hiked from Morrow back to Loveland, thirteen and a half miles. This is where I sparkled. At mile eleven or twelve, the endurance I'd gained from my previous hikes was on display and we entered Loveland together.

On another day I walked the bike trail by myself north from Morrow for eleven miles. I returned to the car on my bike that I had stashed in the woods earlier. I had ridden this stretch of the bike trail quite often before.

As I passed under the towering Jeremiah Morrow Bridge, a span taking I-71 traffic over the gorge, I noticed the crosses again that were planted to mark where people had jumped. As I thought of why they were there, my throat tightened, as well as my grip on the handlebars. They elicit a much more emotional response from me than they used to. I wonder how long the crosses will affect me like this.

To finish this section, Bonnie and I started at Eden Park at the Ohio River Overlook on a cool day, perfect for hiking. Our thirteen-mile hike through the suburbs of Cincinnati and on to Milford gave us great views of landscaping and architecture. No Hawaiian shave ice that day, but we were rewarded with the scene of our friend Dolores smiling and waving a small American flag. She had come to pick us up and return us to our car. Before that, though, we detoured to Panera Bread. This time your tortoise brother *was* first—first in line.

OVER THE LAST COUPLE OF DECADES I have purchased three bicycles, all of them Huffys. I never knew what waves I might create when one of them would travel with me to West Virginia.

My oldest Huffy never did make the trip. It was the one I picked up at an antique car swap meet. I couldn't afford a classic car that day, but how could I pass up a classic Huffy? With only one speed and no hand brakes, though, it has been relegated to an occasional trip to the city park.

I also own a stealthy black Huffy with large letters announcing that it is a STALKER. Dave usually looked up to his older brother, but not when I prowled the hills around Huntington on *that* bike. I learned not to take it down to his house or I would be "stalking" by myself.

One day I hit the jackpot at a local discount store. Right inside the front door was a lineup of ten neon green Huffys. The price tags read $50 each. How many should I buy? No one else I knew needed a bike. I knew for sure that Dave didn't want one. I had two Huffys already, but this deal couldn't be passed up. I purchased the most perfect one and got out quickly before I bought the fleet.

When Dave saw my new machine, his mouth dropped open. He had given my other Huffy an inordinate amount of attention, and I expected no less from him when he got a look at my new pride and joy. My role in such scenarios was always to take him seriously.

"Where did you get *these* wheels?" Dave was finally able to say.

"Mazel's," I replied, "but they are out of them now."

He pressed harder. "Must have been expensive."

"Of course it was, but you have to pay to ride the best."

"Aren't you afraid that it will get stolen or stripped?"

"Sure I am. Wouldn't you be?"

Our verbal sparring was great fun. I would come to the defense of my little green machine quite often. I was determined to prove that it could do anything Dave's bike could. Actually, however, I had to work extremely hard just to keep up and to make it look effortless.

One day, after fifty miles of pedaling along the Greenbrier River Trail, I was a little huffy too. Dave had really gotten ahead of me this time. The last three miles wound up the mountain to the cabin. When I finally pedaled in, he was in the lawn chair, coffee brewed, reading Steinbeck.

"Hey Squooge, why is your face red?" he offered.

"Must be sunburn."

"You seem to be breathing a little hard."

"Just trying to get my money's worth of this mountain air."

I know this game is kind of silly, but I think every good relationship has its share of goofiness. Some of the silliest things are the very things that I remember most fondly about Dave, and miss the most.

Even in the midst of those fond memories, though, feelings of resentment still take me by surprise. I wonder why he cut out on me. Didn't he realize the ripple effects of his planned demise? I have a multitude of emotions concerning Dave. At least time has helped me to sort them out a bit and acknowledge them. It is all part of my grieving process. It's OK to admit that I am still a little "huffy" at times.

ST. MARYS SECTION

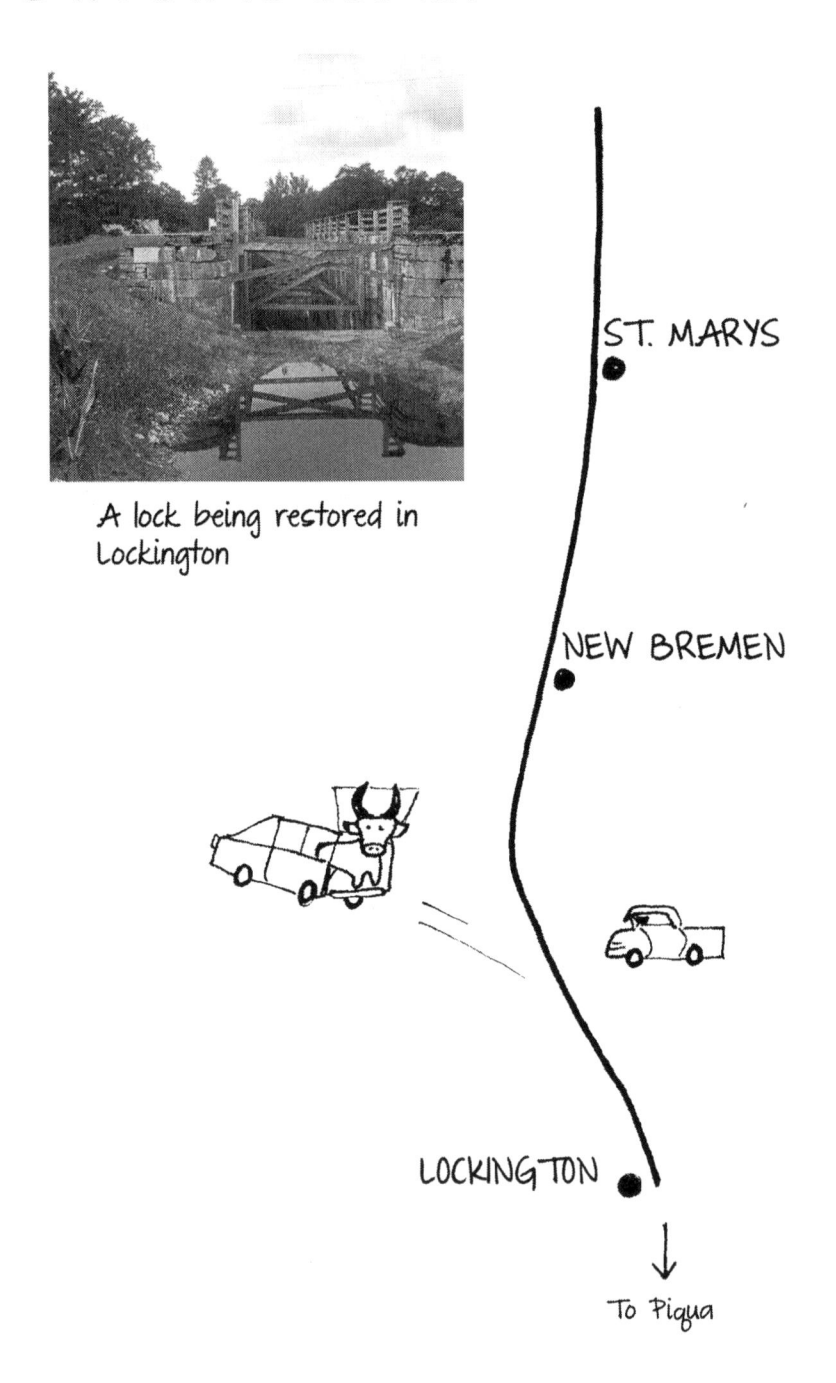

A lock being restored in Lockington

ST. MARYS

NEW BREMEN

LOCKINGTON

↓
To Piqua

Journal Entry #5

Finding a Way to Get Over It

I met up with Charles, whom I knew from my first BT trip, while the August morning still felt comfortable. Arriving that early was quite a feat considering the substantial drive we each had to make from home. Our meeting place was north of Lockington in the St. Marys section.

We left my Caravan off the road on a gravel path at the entrance to a large cornfield, making sure to leave room for a tractor to get by into the field if the need arose. Not the best parking spot, but we really didn't anticipate any problems. I left the usual "Hiking on the Buckeye Trail—Be Back Soon" sign in the window, hopped into Charles's SUV, and rode off to our starting point 11.6 trail miles away in Piqua.

The morning was beautiful with bright blue skies and a decent breeze. We began walking the seven miles back toward Lockington. (These miles were actually part of the Troy section.) Much of the scenery was old canal beds. Even though the canal has been restored to a state of operation at Johnston Farm & Indian Agency in Piqua, we found that much of the canal bed along the trail was filling with dirt and thus fading from view. I admired the stonework of the inoperable locks we passed, chiseled more than a century and a half ago.

By noon, we had passed the sign that welcomed us to Lockington. The mayor, out for his daily walk, greeted us warmly. If he would have been mayor 175 years ago, when the town was called Locksport, he would have done a superb job of welcoming the canal workers with his inviting personality. I wouldn't have hesitated to sign on. He was more than happy to talk to Charles and me about the treasures located in his village.

One thing that makes Lockington so special is its series of six locks that raised canal boats 67 feet to get over the Loramie Summit. The 21-mile-long summit extends from Lockington north to New Bremen. The Miami and Erie Canal builders did not let this obstacle stop them from connecting the Ohio River to Lake Erie. The mayor was impressed with their ingenuity and proud that remnants of their work remain in his town.

After our informative tour, we bade him farewell and proceeded through Lockington Reserve, admiring its canal artifacts. Though most of the St. Marys section follows the canal towpath, we returned to country roads for the last leg of that day's hike. I was tired and looking forward to reaching my car.

When we were about half a mile from said vehicle, facing what little traffic happened by and ready to call it a day, a large pickup truck pulled over in front of us and blocked our path. Even though it was Sunday, it didn't look as if the driver of the truck was on his way to or from church.

He rolled down his window and asked, "Are you from Kentucky?"

For once, I actually wished that I was from West Virginia. Charles looked at me, and the farmer's eyes followed. I raised my hand when I couldn't think of any way to lie out of it.

"Why did you park on my land?" he asked, now that he knew whom to address.

It did not seem to me to be the time to get into the technicalities of right-of-ways. I don't think they mattered much to the farmer at that moment. It appeared that he wanted a target at which to direct his anger. He informed us that he had called the sheriff, so he had already made up his mind that we were up to no good. People had been stealing from his farm and he had had enough.

Charles spoke for us. He didn't argue, but simply explained that we were hiking the Buckeye Trail and that we needed a place to leave the car. We were hikers, not thieves.

After he and the farmer talked for a few minutes, the farmer got his composure back. Charles never lost his. Charles didn't apologize—we hadn't done anything wrong—but he showed empathy for the farmer's situation and listened to his concerns.

The farmer finally started up his truck, not smiling, but apparently ready to let us loose (maybe to give the sheriff a turn at us). I was definitely ready to get out of there. But then Charles said that he had a question for the farmer.

Please Lord, don't let him turn the motor off again.

I held my breath as Charles asked if we could park in the same spot again in a few weeks on the next leg of our hike. The farmer didn't seem too excited by that prospect, but to my amazement he said yes. He just asked that we call and leave a message before we came back. Then he gave us his number and went on his way.

It became clear to me that Charles knew how to handle conflict. He not only defused a tense situation; we even got a favor out of it. If they could bottle that, I'd buy as much as I could afford. Seems like most times you and I would do anything to avoid conflict, and that could sure wear a person out.

As Charles and I began walking the rest of the way to the car, I looked over my shoulder a time or two for the sheriff. When it looked as if he wasn't going to show, I began joking about the situation: What did he think we were planning? To load a cow into the back of my Caravan and haul it back to Kentucky? Did that guy really think he scared us?

We made it to the car and headed back to the other vehicle where Charles and I parted ways.

As I drove south, I thought again of the lock we had seen earlier that day that was in the process of being restored. Sometimes I wish that the entire canal would be restored. I imagined taking a "cruise" from Lake Erie to the Ohio River on a canal boat towed by horses or mules. I read on a plaque that they traveled only four to seven miles per hour. What would I do with all that time?

I wonder if there were any rules against trolling from the back of the boat . . .

THE MEN IN MY FAMILY had a tradition of going to Rice Lake in Ontario every summer. It started with Dad, my brothers Lloyd and Dave, and me. Years later my sons joined us.

One year Dave introduced me to a new fishing tool after we had motored out into deep water.

"What's that?" I gasped as he injected air into the worm's rear quarter, forming a grape-sized bubble.

"My trusty new worm blower."

"Like that done to you?"

"Might not be so bad," Dave decided.

"I wouldn't do that to mine."

"Yeah, you just drown 'em."

Dave religiously followed the bass magazine procedure, and I have to admit that he was rewarded with many bass and walleyes. One day he was having more trouble than usual reeling in his catch. A big muskie just happened to like the look of his blown worm.

I dutifully remarked, "Throw it back, Dave."

"Why?"

"No muskie tag."

"We'll go get one."

"Too late. Already caught it."

We argued until the muskie was barely flopping.

Dave quipped, "Might as well keep him now. He's gonna die anyway."

"I'm not eatin' any," I shot back.

"Suit yourself. More for me."

When we got back to the cabin, Dave cleaned the muskie and put the fillets in the fridge. We didn't talk to each other the rest of the day. We just worked to see who could give the other the coldest shoulder. This passive-aggressive approach was often used in Part A of our conflict resolution. I guess we both thought we could outdo the other one. It never worked, but we sure tried it enough times.

The next morning Dave fried up his fillets and said that I should eat a piece. That was right before I stormed out. This was the typical Part B of the process and would bring the cold-shoulder portion to a dramatic end. While the dishes rattled from the slammed door, the rest of my family probably shook their heads and wondered how long it would take me to come back in.

A half hour later Part C was initiated when I slinked back in, pulled up to the table, and became the first to break the silence.

"How 'bout a piece of that?" I asked, as if no problem had ever existed.

"Sorry I got mad," Dave returned.

"Me too. Fish isn't that bad."

Actually, it wasn't the greatest. I liked the bass and walleye much better, but that didn't matter. We were friends again.

Later that day we both bought a muskie tag, a stamp which added $15 to the cost of each license and probably guaranteed that we had caught our last, and happily headed back out into deep waters in our little craft. I thought I might even go look for my own worm blower on our next trip to Walmart.

DELPHOS SECTION

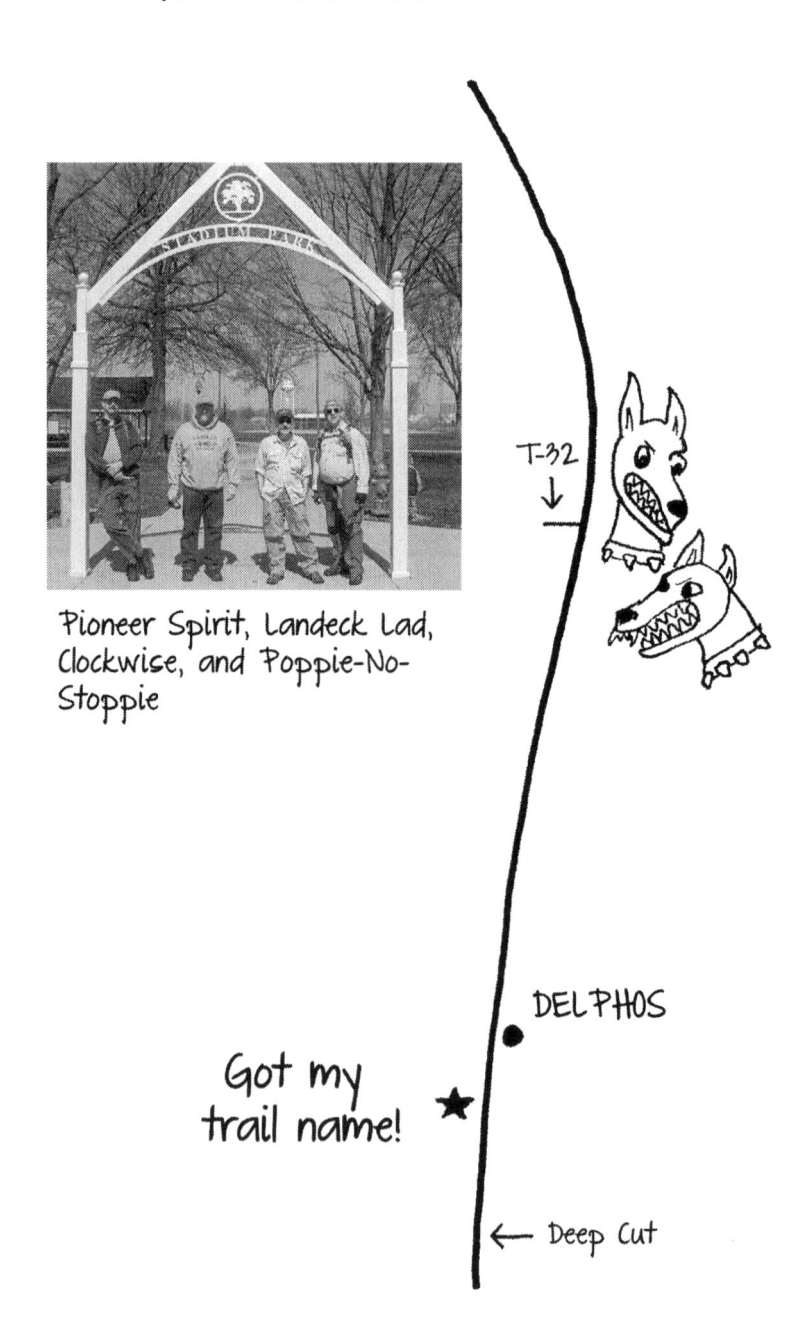

Pioneer Spirit, Landeck Lad, Clockwise, and Poppie-No-Stoppie

T-32 ↓

DELPHOS

Got my trail name! ★

← Deep Cut

Journal Entry #6

Finding a Trail Name

I noticed an advertisement on the BT website for a hike in the Delphos section. Since I hadn't hiked there yet, I eagerly signed up. I was glad I did. I not only completed some miles, but I also made some new friends. Poppie had organized the hike. Sam and Richard (aka Landeck Lad and Pioneer Spirit respectively) also signed up, making it a foursome.

The wind blew steadily at about 30 mph as we hiked counterclockwise (south) along the flat towpath. Sam lives near there in the town of Landeck and helps maintain the trail. Fortunately for us, he also knows quite a bit about the canal and was willing to share a good history lesson.

As we trudged forward, we walked into a cut in the hill. The windy plains gave way to a windy tunnel. Straining to be heard above the squall, Sam explained that we were traversing the Deep Cut, a gulley—6,600 feet long and ranging from 5 to 52 feet deep—cut entirely by hand. Laborers were paid 30 cents per day plus a jigger of whiskey to dig it. I guess it was worth it since it saved having to build locks to hoist the boats over the hill. Having to construct another Lockington would have made a deep cut into the coffers of the builder, the fledgling new state of Ohio.

I wished that the *wind* would become history. I wondered if they ever put the horses or mules on the boat and raised some sails on a day like this. The wind made each mile seem like two (I considered writing forty miles down in my mileage log that night). I complained to Poppie quite a few times about the counterclockwise direction we were going since he was the one who had organized the hike. The wind didn't seem to faze him.

"You ought to be called 'Poppie-no-Stoppie,'" I whined.

He shot back, "You ought to be called 'Clockwise.'"

Not bad since my initials happen to be CW.

That evening, a gracious local businessman in Delphos took all four of us out and footed the bill for a great supper. We were thankful: we had had enough footing for the day. When introducing ourselves, Poppie ventured his new name, "Poppie-no-Stoppie?" Nobody laughed, so I bravely followed his lead and said, "Clockwise." Poppie and I were now linked with other great hikers, from Captain Blue to Worldwalker—we had trail names!

Hoping that my new name carried some clout, I lobbied Poppie to change the direction to clockwise for the next day's hike. I figured that way we would avoid walking into the wind that was expected to continue. He reluctantly agreed, and the next morning we proceeded to shuttle the vehicles into place.

The wind that day seemed to have relented only a little, dropping to around 25 mph. We set out to the north. I realized quickly that we again faced the wind. *How can this be? Maybe they won't notice if I don't mention it.* No such luck. Sherlock-no-Stoppie detected the change quickly and wasted no time in pointing it out to me.

I was lucky not to have been named Whiner the day before, so I took the ribbing from the guys and fell in close behind to block the wind, secretly becoming The Drafter. In spite of the atmospheric opposition, we completed 21 more miles that day for a two-day total of 41.

□ □ □

Even though we had covered a lot of ground on that first hike, 22 miles of the northern part of the section remained for me. Due to a lingering case of severe plantar fasciitis, I was forced to forgo two great chances to hike it, both with Poppie. Months later when the inflammation began to subside, so, it seemed, did the chance that I would find anyone else to hike it with.

I had considered riding my Huffy the remaining miles and calling it done. That sounded like a workable plan until I visualized myself having to someday explain why I didn't actually *walk* all of the BT. Yes, Huffys require foot power, but for me it doesn't count unless it's "boots on the ground."

I did come up with a solution, however. To pull it off, I found a place to stash my bike, parked my car about five miles up the trail, then walked back to my bike. Using this system, I was able to knock off twelve miles the first day in that flat countryside. I got my miles in and a double dose of exercise, plus I passed friendly faces multiple times.

Unfortunately, not all the faces looked quite so friendly the next day. As I pedaled past a yard as long as a football field, I couldn't help but notice the twin Dobermans that matched the speed of my bike. A lot of teeth were showing, but my guess was that it was not smiles revealing them. Fortunately, the dogs kept their teeth in the yard.

Thank you God for the inventor of the invisible fence.

After making it past unscathed, it only took a minute or two for it to dawn on me that the next step of my great plan would require me to walk back past those two cloned canines. Would they risk a slight shock for some juicy hiker bites? Your brave big brother decided not to find out.

On the walk back I studied the map. I decided to pass a turn blaze, this time on purpose, and cut back over to the trail on T-32. That would leave me with about a mile of the

BT that was only biked, but I would also avoid the Dobermans, thus making it possible to hike another day.

When I got to T-32, I could hardly believe it even showed up on my map. A big green road sign marked only a set of tire tracks running through a huge hayfield. Then I remembered some of the township roads in southern Ohio—one that even followed down the bed of a stream—and I realized that this could actually be the "road." I trudged forward, heavy with the knowledge that I was off the trail. I walked about a half mile, eager to get back on the BT.

Everything seemed fine until I saw where the road had taken me. Imagine the *dogs'* surprise when I appeared again —this time wheel-less and right in their side yard. Their jaws dropped, but only for a moment. Fortunately more invisible fence was buried between them and me (probably to protect them from the heavy traffic driving across the hayfield). Once again, they stayed in the yard while I scurried ahead, feeling like Daniel escaping the lions' den.

That wasn't the first time I had read a map wrong, or that invisible forces had kept me safe. If I hadn't already been dubbed Clockwise, I would probably have changed my name then and there to Daniel the Second.

D AVE AND I MET SOME COOL CHARACTERS during our limited time on the AT, including Caveman and Kitchen Sink. No doubt they were named by other hikers. We thought their names were perfect. It was obvious that Kitchen Sink carried everything (well, almost). Caveman, on the other hand, had a different plan called "I have no equipment or supplies, but I can charm my way along." I related to Kitchen Sink more since I was the one who had packed the iron skillet; Dave leaned more toward Caveman because of the charm factor. Dave and I never did get trail names for ourselves back then, at least not ones that stuck. (Someone must have already claimed "Ironman.")

If we had thru-hiked the AT, I can imagine Dave giving me a fitting trail name—maybe something like Goody Thru-Shoes. I could be a little legalistic back in the day. That moniker would have probably irked me at the time. Now I can see the humor in the name. Today I am a little less into the law and a little more into God's grace. That tends to balance out the scales for me.

I guess now it's up to me to give Dave *his* trail name. After considerable thought, I believe I've come up with the perfect one: Thoreau-hiker. I'm sure he would have approved, as much as he loved to soak in the writings of the New England Transcendentalists. Dave was always looking for someone who was into his mentors—Thoreau, Emerson, and the rest—to share an intellectual conversation with. That was never me.

One thing I did know about Thoreau was that, while he lived simply, he made every effort to live life fully. Dave seemed content with his modest home and possessions, but at the same time he would heartily immerse himself in any activity he chose to do. I think of his vacation to Jamaica where, instead of visiting the usual tourist traps, he spent his time with the natives to get the full experience. He was always asking me what I wanted from life and what I was doing to get it. Sometimes he made fun of my Protestant work ethic. I *could* get pretty wrapped up in making a living and miss life going by. Dave would be happy to know that retirement has more than released the stranglehold that ethic had on me.

I found that Thoreau had deep-felt beliefs that he wasn't afraid to express. For example, to protest the Mexican-American War, Thoreau refused to pay a tax. Also, he uncompromisingly defended John Brown while some of his contemporaries feared to. Dave stuck to his personal beliefs as well, even when they weren't popular with family and friends. Not everyone in his circle was as progressive in their politics as he was. He didn't always see the Christian faith the same way as his peers, either. He pressed me to formulate and express my views. I actually had to change a few that didn't hold water.

I also discovered that Thoreau traveled the world via his reading. Dave was definitely a kindred spirit. All I have to do to prove that is to think of him in his Lazy Boy with a work of classic literature in his lap. Depending on the book he was reading, he could fly cheaply back in time or across the world with plenty of leg room and no jet lag.

Another similarity between Dave and Thoreau was quite unsettling for me. I had to swallow a lump in my throat when I discovered that Thoreau left Walden Pond in 1846 and traveled to Mt. Katahdin in Maine. That peak just happens to be the northern terminus of the AT. Tears formed when I read that the deep wilderness he encountered on his journey gave him some added appreciation of the civilization he had distanced himself from. He found balance.

Maybe Dave was looking for balance in his wilderness retreats. Maybe Thoreau-hiker would have found a needed stability had we been able to take that trip we talked about.

WILLIAMSBURG SECTION

Starting my solo hike from Lake Grant

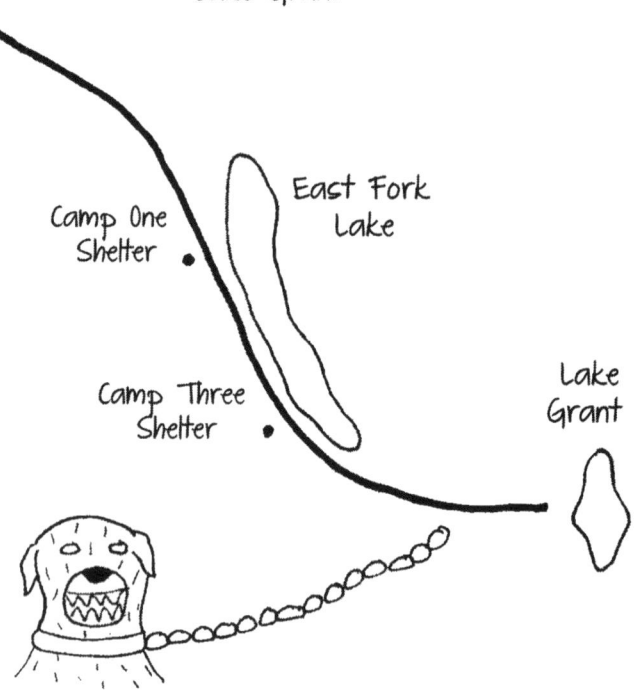

East Fork Lake

Camp One Shelter

Camp Three Shelter

Lake Grant

Journal Entry #7

Finding Shelter

Fourteen wide eyes peered out from the back wall of the three-sided shelter, watching the flashing night sky. Rain had followed wind which had followed thunder which had followed lightning. What would follow next?

Distant tornado sirens announced the presence of a swirling funnel. Was it headed our way? Would we be pulled out of our hut and hurled into the next county?

Eyes grew even wider as rapid-fire pounding suddenly began on the roof, overpowering the clapping of the thunder and the whistling of the wind. We were being bombarded by quarter-sized hail. Seven souls were grateful that the powers-that-be at East Fork had built this hut at Camp One.

OK, Dave, at this point you would probably be wondering whether I have joined a hiking club or a drama club. Well, I paid my $20 to join the Buckeye Trail Association; the drama was thrown in for free.

Bonnie had dropped me off two mornings earlier at Lake Grant, located at the east end of the Williamsburg section. I had been planning this hike for several weeks. It would be my longest solo hike on the BT so far. As I left her to hit the road, I assured her one last time that this would be safe (she doesn't like for me to hike alone), and probably even boring.

I had ten road miles to walk until I would enter the woods at East Fork State Park, and then another seven miles or so to Camp Three. Even though I hadn't started until ten that morning, I figured that I would easily arrive well before dark, which would be around nine o'clock.

The hike started to become less routine when I happened upon the dog at mile seven—a dog that wanted to add a little drama to my day. It wasn't *all* bad: the dog was chained. But it was *mostly* bad: one end of the chain was trailing on the ground. I guess in a weird sort of way you could call him a "trail dog." However, his temperament was not exactly like the congenial dogs you and I met on the AT. Looks like drama time.

> There I was, with nothing between this carnivorous canine and me but 15 to 20 feet of open space, and the distance was slowly closing. Unlike most of the pesky dogs that just wanted to harass hikers, this one was not bounding, bouncing, or barking. Rather, he was inching toward me in a low crouch with a guttural growl and bared teeth. It was time for action—but what kind of action?
>
> I could pop open my umbrella, being sure to make a loud snap with it. I had been told that this might startle a dog, and if not, at least provide a barrier that would slow down the attack. However, since the day was fair, the umbrella was stashed deep in my pack. No time-outs here.
>
> What about the spray? I may get it out in time, but should I actually use it? The label had

warned against using it on highly motivated dogs. I wasn't positive, but I thought that it was safe to assume that if this dog had mustered enough motivation to break a decent-sized chain, he probably had plenty left over for me. Nix the spray.

I had heard that I should avoid eye contact and back away carefully in a situation such as this. Maybe a good idea if the chain was still attached to the doghouse, or if the perp was not still slinking his way toward me.

I finally realized that this was a face-off, so I ignored the no eye contact advice: I stared right into his hungry orbs and yelled "NO!" Now, I'm not recommending this. I was surprised that I was standing this strong. I guess the dog was, too, because his now creeping advance ceased. I turned and eased away without looking back, and was immensely relieved that the growl wasn't following me.

Gradually I picked up my pace so he wouldn't have too much time to think it over. I whispered many prayers of thanks before I finally hit the woods in mid-afternoon.

A new obstacle quickly loomed before me—and under me: ankle deep mud, churned over and over by horses, aggravated by a wetter-than-usual spring season. I was lucky to get in a mile every hour.

I arrived at Camp Three just as the last light of day was fading. Even though I was dog-tired, I still took the time to pitch my tent. Nearby was an empty shelter. Though I didn't need it, it was comforting to know that it was available.

Feeling fairly rested the next morning, I set out, wet boots and all. At least I wouldn't have to worry any more about trying to keep my feet dry. I had all day to hike the ten miles to Camp One, so I took it easy, enjoying the gorges, swamps, lake views, and grassy areas East Fork has to offer. When I rolled into camp, I was eager to hydrate my meal and dehydrate my boots.

Four tents eventually occupied the campsite. My fellow campers and I planned to use the shelter only as a dry storage place for our packs. As darkness crept in, we began to tighten our circle around the community fire, sipping and sharing together as the flames engulfed the wood and danced toward the sky.

That is, until lightning announced the evening's unexpected entertainment.

> Soon the sky yielded up the storm, sending us racing for cover. There we were, peering out of shelter one. Objects not secured blew across the opening like tumbleweeds. Some of the icy missiles ricocheted into our refuge, sending us closer to the back wall. Brilliant flashes of lightning illuminated our wind-distended tents, which were being tested to new limits. Trees bent over as if to lie low until the raging wind was past, not reverting to their stately upright posture until the storm had moved east.

In a short time, calm returned. We lingered in the shelter to conduct a post-storm analysis and to enjoy the new camaraderie and common bond among us. Eventually we worked our way back to our individual sites, each surprised to find tents intact and dry inside.

The storm had forced all of us to leave our comfort zones and come together—like the storms of life did on more than one occasion for you and me.

DAVE WAS ALWAYS THE ADVENTURER of the family; I, the cautious one. However, you wouldn't know who was who if you heard us bragging on the trail. Especially when it came to bears. We both talked big, but our actions revealed otherwise.

On the AT, we happened upon a lone hiker who told us of the eight bears he had spotted during his trek through Shenandoah. Some of them he had actually encountered. One bear, which was "as big as a jeep," had met him as they each rounded a sharp bend. Both walkers were equally startled; luckily it was the *bear* that had the sense to run.

We walked that day with our new hero, and we logically named him Eight Bear. Although we told him that we wished we could have been with him when he hiked with the shaggy omnivores, we were lying like bearskin rugs.

On day two, we realized that bears must really like Eight Bear, maybe as much as we did. That morning we managed to distance ourselves from him. We didn't want to part with him as Nine Bear.

The next night, while huddled in a shelter, there was more bear talk. A thru-hiker traveling the opposite direction said that a bear had approached the last hut just the night before. There he was, within 30 feet of the shelter, up on his hind legs and roaring. Luckily the hiker's trail dog barked and discouraged the bear from staying for supper.

As we headed north the next morning, Dave noted that we were bound for that very shelter. We were walking by ourselves at the time, but we figured that a crowd would materialize after we settled in for the evening.

That night when darkness fell, the shelter remained illuminated by our larger-than-normal fire, one we hoped would soon draw in the usual collection of thru-hikers. Despite our prayers, though, we heard no reinforcements coming. We heard only some stirring in the brush.

"I doubt if that's a bear," I said. "That trail dog probably scared him into the next territory."

"I wish *we* had a dog," Dave replied.

"If it is that bear, I doubt that he will approach the hut again."

"Especially since the fire is eight feet high."

"Are you scared?"

"No. See those picnic tables?"

In a matter of moments we had two of the heavy wooden structures turned sideways to make the fourth wall of the shelter, forming a "bear-ier." I'm sure the bear could have climbed over the tables, but at least we were going to make him work for his meal.

WEST UNION SECTION

Lake Grant

Back road nativity

Mo-o-o-o-ot

Rock ledge

Ohio River

Journal Entry #8

Finding the Shepherd

The West Union section starts out with some serious hills, but eventually it becomes more flatlander friendly. In one spot, the Ohio River flows only two miles away. Over 99 percent of this section is on back roads, alongside which are many cool-looking barns, eye-catching stone walls, and picturesque streams.

I hiked one of those pleasant, scenic byways with Bob on a frosty day. It was well into the morning of New Year's Eve eve, and we hadn't been passed by the last hour's motorist yet. With so little traffic out there, it was easy to get lost in thought.

I evaluated my journey up to that point. I had finished most of this section in four previous hikes. The twelve miles that day would complete not only the West Union section, but quite a nice chunk of the BT. Not bad for my first eight months on the trail. If I didn't get run over first, that is. I scooted out of the middle of the road when a pickup approached. We tended to get careless on those quiet back roads.

The year was ending with a weight on my shoulders—the unwanted load of the sad and painful memories of you and Mark—even though all I physically carried was a light day pack. The holiday season brought mixed emotions as I remembered past Christmases with you guys. I thought of the miles that still lay before me through Shawnee near our Day Hike Trail and near the finish line in Troy where your nephew and my son's gravestone marks his resting place. My steps became heavier.

I steered my mind back to my hike. I have to admit that section hiking is working out OK. Thru-hiking sounds manlier, I know. But when I sat for hours with maps, paper, and pencil, I realized that too many arrangements had to be made in advance, such as where I would spend the nights. There weren't enough campgrounds around, at least not in the right places, so I would have to be mentally ready to stealth-camp. Maybe when I was in college I would have sneaked into a cornfield and taken up residence for the night, but these days I prefer for someone to know where I'm camping, and to say it's OK. I guess I just don't want to take the risks I used to.

One risk that might have paid off would have been to refuse to leave when you sent me home at the end of that weekend. Maybe you hoped that I would intervene, Dave. Or was your plan set in stone when you phoned me to come? This is the question that just won't let go of me, whether I'm on the trail or sitting at my desk writing.

I caught up with Bob, and we eventually delved into the subject of politics. Though the 2010 midterm elections are still almost a year down the road, predictions are already being made about who will be the republican candidate for the next presidential election.

As you know, sometimes I don't do well at debating issues, so I enjoy talking politics with like-minded people such as Bob. That day, however, I ventured out of my comfort zone to broach the subject with the cows we passed, not knowing their political leanings.

We decided to conduct a straw poll to get their grass roots opinions. We asked the cows whom they liked for the next presidential candidate. Never having studied any bovine languages, though, we weren't sure if they were voicing support for *Moo*chele Bachmann, *Moo*t Gingrich, or *Moo*t Romney. They all sounded alike to us. Maybe on the next hike we'll conduct a "gallop" poll with some of the horses we see.

When Bob and the cows got tired of politics, I finally got to wondering who was tending all the creatures we saw in the fields that day. No one at all was outside. Seemed like we would have seen *someone* in four hours. After all, we'd passed nine houses.

That is when our journey brought us to a nativity scene. We saw the statues nestled under a rock ledge on that back road. It was the last place I expected to find Him. But there was Jesus, away from the noise, the traffic, and the lights. There He was, surrounded by the four-legged creatures in the fields. There was the Great Tender, watching over all His creation, and bringing comfort to me.

Goes to show, you never know whom you will run into on the Buckeye Trail.

IT'S SUPER TUESDAY. I don't know why, but I keep getting political calls this morning. Our state doesn't even have its primary today. I recognize the numbers on caller ID, and I don't answer. I am trying to do some writing, and the ringing phone is a distraction. It's not that I don't care about the primaries; I just hate to see the candidates eating each other alive.

Dave and I almost never agreed on politics. When I wasn't able to steer a conversation away from the subject, Dave would steer it—to the left.

Perhaps the only political issue that we agreed on was the right to bear arms, so that was one subject of conversation that usually went more smoothly. Not that guns were numerous in our family. Dad never did have guns around the house, at least that I can remember. He probably had more than his fill of them during his service as a Ranger in World War II.

I have owned guns, but only for brief seasons of my life. The first was at the age of 12 when I received a Daisy BB gun for Christmas. I was overjoyed despite the fact that Mom and Dad passed a flurry of gun controls on it in a very bipartisan manner.

I was almost as happy when my friend Roy received one the following year. He must not have gotten the same lecture as I did because as I was climbing a tree in his backyard on that Christmas Day, he decided to test his new weapon's accuracy on my eyelid. The shot startled me, causing me to lose my balance and fall.

The entire town of Tippecanoe must have heard me yelling. Roy's dad appeared and probably saved my other eyelid by breaking Roy's gun over his knee. When I got home I received a little sympathy, but then I lost *my* gun as well, at least until the gun controls could be further evaluated.

Years later when I was away at college, a buddy borrowed money from me. Wanting to pay me back but not having the cash, he repaid me with a .22 caliber rifle. Unfortunately, it didn't come with a common sense manual.

One day I took my new weapon and went for a walk along some back roads. I shot at a few cans until I tired of that. Then I spotted an old, disintegrating trailer with its windows broken out. I took a quick shot at its wall, attempting to imitate the Rifleman. Sure enough, I hit the structure through the overgrowth and vines clinging to its sides.

While I was still congratulating myself on marksmanship and style, an angry occupant appeared at the opening where the door used to hang. I was horrified—and unbelievably relieved that I hadn't hit him. I was also fortunate that *he* didn't have a weapon. He angrily asked my name so he could report the incident to the police. Though not proud of my response, I gave him a false name and hurried off, still shaken. After that fiasco, I confiscated my own gun. The Rifleman I wasn't.

Dave was over 40 when he bought the first and only gun that I was aware of, so I figured he was old enough to have more sense than I had displayed with mine. He told me that it was for self-defense. Since his house was in a rural location, I didn't give it a second thought—at least not for quite some time.

It was probably a good thing that we didn't own guns, as intensely as we disagreed on other political issues. When Dave wanted to tick me off, he pulled out his list of ten words: Bush, Cheney, Rummy, Brownie, Iraq, Blackwater, Mission Accomplished, Gitmo, WMD'S, and *Haliburton*. Good words, I thought, but not the way he used them.

I'd like to think that if Dave and I were hiking now, I would be the Great Debater, skillfully defending every candidate and cause that I believe in. No more quiet fuming while Dave sarcastically scalds my heroes in D.C. I might even come up with a list of ten words for *him*.

On the other hand, maybe we would have moved beyond our political differences to a more peaceful place. In the end, it was our relationship that mattered, not our politics. The folks I saw under a ledge while I was hiking on a back road one day reminded me of that.

BURTON SECTION

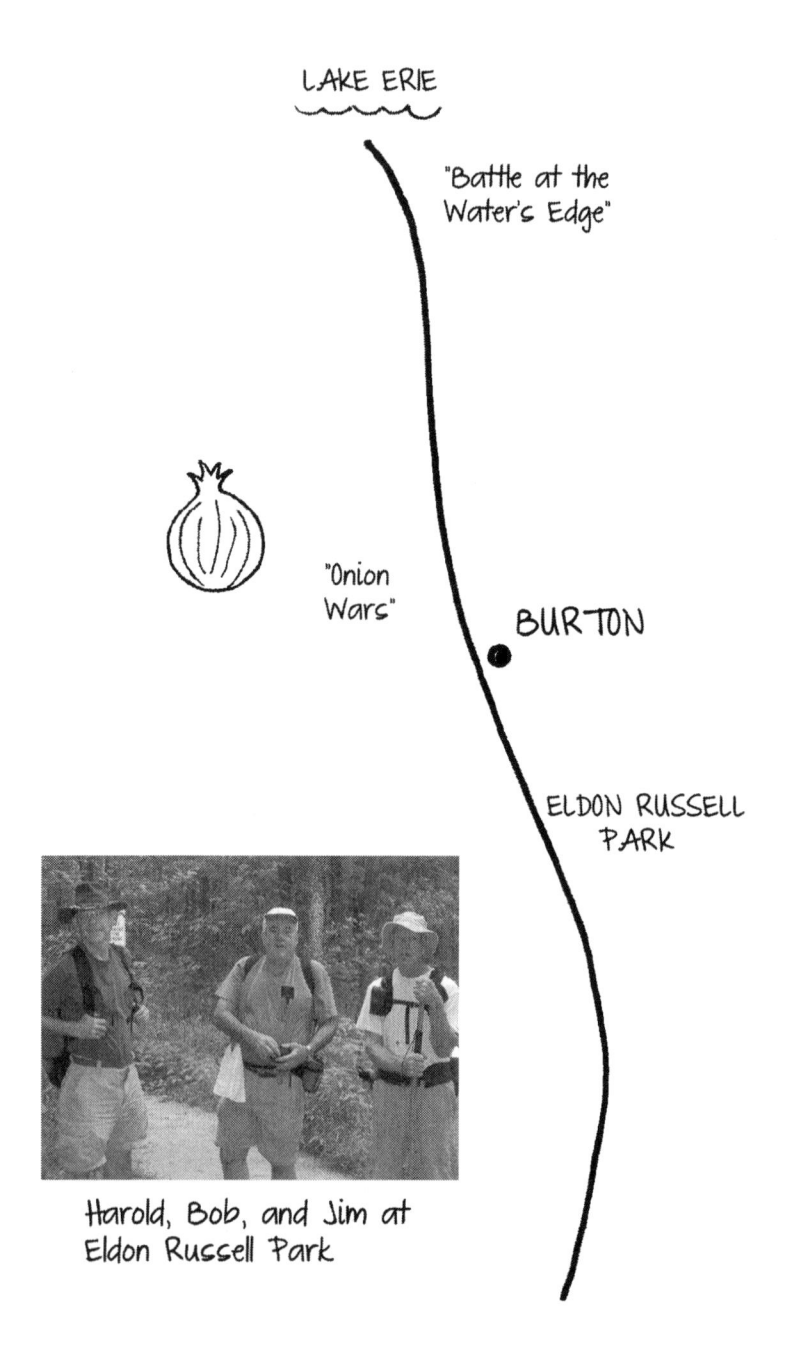

LAKE ERIE

"Battle at the Water's Edge"

"Onion Wars"

BURTON

ELDON RUSSELL PARK

Harold, Bob, and Jim at Eldon Russell Park

Journal Entry #9

Finding a Good Book

Waves broke against the Lake Erie shore. Two hardened, determined travelers—some might say drifters—met at the water's edge to settle a score once and for all. Gulls circled overhead. They seemed to sense the drama that was unfolding. If you listened carefully, you could almost hear the "Wah-WAH-wah" of a spaghetti western.

Bob tightened his belt; Harold loosened a strap. A click. Then a long second of silence . . . Harold quickly reached. So did Bob, but a split second slower.

Bob, face contorted, grabbed at his throat and choked. "That thar was the lousiest draw I've had on the en-tire trail," he said as he spit out the water and put the bottle back in its holder.

Harold replied, "Mine's fresh. Take a draw. You'll need it today, pardner. I guarantee you."

That's *kind* of how it started that morning in the Burton section. I exaggerated a bit for entertainment purposes because I know how much you *love* westerns, Dave. (Almost as much as you love Huffys.)

However, the situation was real. Harsh sentiments, spoken and unspoken, had been festering between those two for over a year. The conflict started when Bob had to go home early from a previous hike and Harold had questioned his ability to last it out. Them thar's fightin' words fer hikers.

Those men would duel it out that day—not with pistols, but with boots—to see who could out-hike the other. They were working it out the Old West way, physically instead of verbally, the way you and I did a time or two. Jim and I cheered them on as they disappeared down the trail.

That trail had hosted another battle many years ago, today referred to as the Onion Wars. In 1901, a resident of Burton tampered with the flow of the Cuyahoga River in order to do some major onion farming. When this alone didn't work, he hired some roughnecks to blow up a rock dam that was impeding the flow of the river. However, a group of shotgun-toting townspeople chased them off with blasts of rock salt, ending the Onion Wars. Guess those "bad guys" didn't want to add any more sodium to their diets.

Jim and I enjoyed this section with its beautiful parks, New England style towns, and scenic back roads. We didn't know how much Bob and Harold saw at the pace they were going. We just knew that when we reached camp each day, they had their tent and tarp pitched and the fire blazing.

Like I always told you, Dave, they did it right in the Old West. It looks to me like it still works, judging by the handshake and the looks of new respect between Bob and Harold as they parted ways at the end of the trail.

DAVE AND I BOTH liked to read about horses. The horses in my books bore names like Red or Paint; in Dave's, they would be Rocinante or Pegasus. Mine carried heroes that roped, shot, and sang; Dave's carried imaginative "knights," transported Greek special forces (in their bellies), or brought thunderbolts to Zeus.

Almost without fail, Dave would call a meeting of the West Virginia-Kentucky Book Club when I went to visit. The sessions usually didn't last long. Dave would always begin by asking the same questions about the book I was currently reading, usually in this order:
Has the hero met the girl yet?
Has he lost the girl yet?
Has she lost the ranch yet?
Has he got the girl back yet?
Has she got the ranch back yet?
OK, I guess a certain formula does exist in my books, but maybe that is what appeals to me. Things look good to me in black and white. I like reading over and over that crime doesn't pay and that you can always trust your horse. However, this did not equip me at all in discussing Hemingway or Homer or Whomever, so the meeting would inevitably come to an abrupt and awkward close.

One day at the library, as I passed the classic section on my way to get another Louis L'Amour fix, I grabbed *Don Quixote* from the shelf. I promised myself I would read at least a little so that I could ask Dave a question or two. To my surprise, I found it had more action than most of my westerns. I raced through the book from cover to cover.

The book club was a little more exciting for both of us the next time we met. Dave knew that I had expanded my reading list just so I would have more in common with him. I won't forget that surprised and contented look on his face during the entire discussion. The whole visit was more fun, and when I jumped into my car to return home the next day, I was gratified to find a gift on my seat: *Ride the River* by Louis L'Amour! I already had that one, but I didn't tell Dave. I kept it there between the seats for years to come.

NEW STRAITSVILLE SECTION

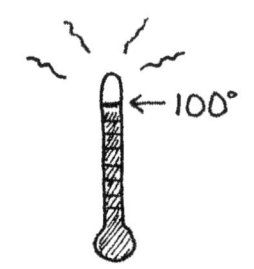

←100°

Me, Jim, and Liz before we knew what we were getting into

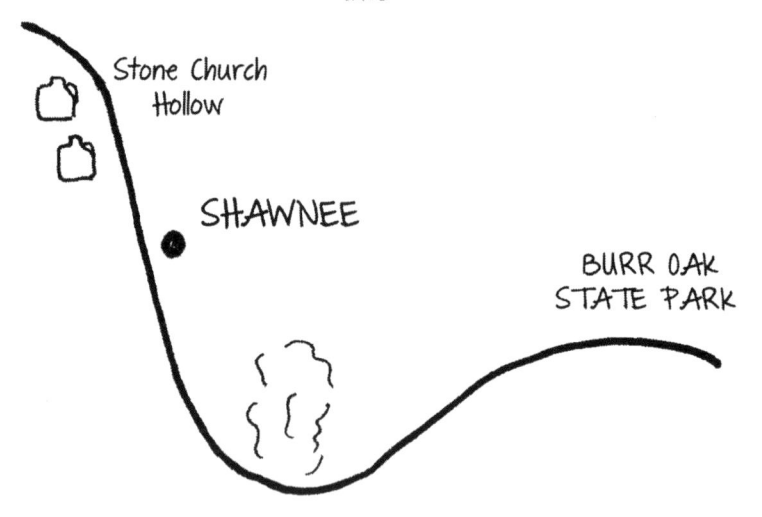

Stone Church Hollow

SHAWNEE

BURR OAK STATE PARK

Smoke Rise Ranch Resort

Journal Entry #10

Losing Brain Cells

My first backpacking trip on the BT had actually ended in the middle of the New Straitsville section. John had informed me before that trip that cigars would be smoked and adult beverages would be consumed during the hike. One reason for the heads up might have been that word had gotten out about me sometimes "preaching" at camper services in a state park. I told John that I didn't indulge, but that I'd be OK with any of the others doing so.

Mrs. Green, my sixth grade teacher, told our class that alcohol kills brain cells. You were only about one year old then, Dave, and didn't need to know yet about neurons and synapses biting the dust. Though I learned a lot from her, my ears were deaf to her advice about alcohol. Some years later I did indeed indulge. I don't know how many cells the alcohol killed, but it definitely made me act stupider when I used it.

A trail angel brought a cooler of beer the night we camped at Burr Oak State Park. I sat on it as we began to swap stories around the campfire. I was sipping up some of the last of my precious coffee supply—"Baptist beer" as you and I used to call it. My caffeine level was getting dangerously low.

A voice from behind startled me. "Wouldn't you know that the Baptist in the group would be sitting on the beer cooler."

"Let's see your ID," I kidded.

I got up, reached into the cooler, and handed a can to Harold. As the night wore on, I tossed a can to anyone who bellied up to the cooler. Funny, a Baptist bartender.

The next day we traveled many hilly miles, so I was glad when Pat announced that our camp was on the hilltop ahead. I had to blink in amazement when we came upon Smoke Rise Ranch Resort. Who would have expected a dude ranch out there in the wilderness. Guests can be cowboys. How cool is that! However, none of our little band had any energy left over for riding or roping; those foothills had given us a workout.

A lot of the smoke I saw rise that night was wafting from glowing cigars. I miss smoking them the most when I am camping. I might have tried one if I was capable of moderation, but just one puff would flip a switch back on that would be almost impossible to shut off. I made myself content with the aroma that drifted my way and slowly drank the last cup of my weak, instant coffee.

The next day we arrived at our final destination, the small town of Shawnee, and stopped at Andrew's office. Andrew is the executive director of the Buckeye Trail Association. He must have sensed my plight because he quickly brewed a pot of coffee and whisked a cup to me to awaken any surviving brain cells.

□ □ □

Some time passed before I was recently able to finish this section. It turned out to be my first endeavor to plan a group hike on the BT. Since I have gained more experience now, I hoped to make a good impression as a planner and leader. Two prospects canceled, but Jim and Liz showed up for the three-day backpacking trip.

After squandering the entire morning stashing several gallon jugs of water every four or five miles and solving some problems involved with permission to park a vehicle at our destination, we were finally ready to depart. Once again, I was in the town of Shawnee.

We met a group of kids and adults involved in a summer program. They were gathered in front of a magnificent building from Shawnee's glory days. As we chatted with them, they expressed amazement that we would actually be hiking 36 miles. I'm sure they had a list of reasons in mind why we shouldn't be hiking that day, some of which we were already painfully aware.

For one thing, we knew that the average high temperature for those three days was expected to be close to 100 degrees. Also, the humidity was soaring. Already the air was so moist that I felt as if I needed floaties. Any more moisture in the air and we would have been dog paddling.

In addition to the oppressive weather conditions, a storm had passed through that area the previous week, a rare "super derecho" on its way from Indiana to Washington, D.C. It's also called a land hurricane, and we could certainly see why. The powerful winds had downed thousands of trees, taking power lines with them, and leaving much of the state without electricity.

There was a third reason not to hike that we hadn't even heard about: due to so many downed trees and power lines, the trails in that part of Wayne Forest were closed to hikers. Um ... that would be us.

Not exactly the perfect hiking conditions.

The temperature had already climbed to 90 degrees when we set off at noon. It took at least four hours to hike the first four miles. Jim estimated that we limboed under, climbed over, or circled around a hundred fallen trees that littered the trail in that distance alone. The biggest drought in decades had dried up many of the streams, but we were able to enjoy our fresh, though hot, stashed water when we took a break at the Stone Church Hollow trailhead. Although Liz was a physically active person, this was her first backpacking trip. What a way to break in. All three of us, though, were hanging in there.

We strapped the empty jugs onto our packs and set off with the hope of reaching camp by dark. It was already half past four, and we still had at least six miles to go, several hills to climb, and who knew how many trees to navigate around. I would have been irked at the planner of the hike and determined to never join another trek led by him, except for the fact that it happened to be me.

As the hour of eight o'clock approached and then became history, we wondered if we would make camp and our next water stash before we lost our light. We decided we would probably have enough water if we couldn't make it, and there were places to pitch a tent. Wayne National Forest allows hikers to set up tents along the trail—when the trails are open!

We staggered ahead trancelike, occasionally groaning as if in mortal agony, not wanting to stop because camp could be just around the next bend. Finally, just as darkness was beginning to fall, we reached our destination. We cooked our meals by flashlight. We likely wouldn't have even needed to heat the water; the temperature was still in the low-to-mid 90s. I was too tired to eat much. I know you won't believe me, but I actually pitched some food.

As I lay sweating in my tent, I figured the hike was doomed. I probably should have canceled three days before when the forecast warned of record heat, but I didn't want to seem wimpy. However, what's worse—Jim and Liz thinking I'm soft, or them thinking my brain is mush?

When I crawled out of my tent the next morning, though, hope was in the air. The slight breeze stirred up pleasant breakfast smells. My companions were refreshed, and so was I. We were grateful that the remaining 26 miles would be road miles, which meant no more downed trees and power lines.

Throughout those last two days, almost as if I had planned it, strangers showed up at the most opportune times with aid and comfort. Chris and Steve gave us juicy apples; Skip provided Gatorade and water; Cheryl produced cold sodas when she found us wilted in front of a given-up-for-dead pop machine; Don tossed us towels and said to dunk our heads under his pump, from which issued icy spring water. All of those kind folks certainly made me look better as the hike organizer.

We reached our car around seven o'clock on day three and headed for the DQ to celebrate surviving the hike. I forget what Jim and Liz ordered, but I refused to settle for anything less than a Blizzard.

Before we parted ways, I asked my hiking companions what they thought of the hike. A dangerous thing to do, I know. But, to my amazement, they both smiled and said they loved it. Maybe the heat had taken a toll on *their* brain cells.

THERE WAS A COMPETITIVE STREAK between Dave and me, but we seldom chose to prove our abilities with normal games like tennis or golf. That was good for me because I wasn't as athletic as Dave. That was good for Dave because he excelled at anything out of the ordinary.

One boring day we came up with a new game: Meet Me at the Rock. The rules were simple. One of us would call the other and pronounce those five words. It didn't matter the time of day or the season of the year. It might happen at two in the morning, or maybe the call would come in the middle of a snowstorm. Theoretically, both of us would immediately begin the trip to Chimney Top Rock in the Daniel Boone National Forest. The callee was to quit whatever he was doing and head for the rock. For me it was 2 hours and 13 minutes away and for Dave it was 2 hours and 18 minutes, so it became a race. However, the rules allowed no speeding.

We schemed to try to catch the other off guard. Dave initiated the game two months after its inception by calling me at school where my students were engaged in some serious frog dissection. The secretary sent an office girl up to my classroom with a note containing only those five panic-inducing words.

I got a call from Dave the next day. "Where were you?"

"Afraid to leave class."

"What's the worst that could've happened?"

"Lose my job, my home, my wife . . ."

"Chicken."

Dave one, me zero.

About a month later it was my turn. I called with the five-word message, quickly hung up, and jumped in my car. As I entered the Red River Gorge and neared Chimney Rock, I became excited. I would beat Dave and even the score.

Well, I did beat Dave. I watched the sun travel across the sky, memorized every tree and rock in the horizon, and left that evening without any sighting of Dave.

I called the next day. "Where were you?"

"Yesterday was the one day of my recent life where I couldn't get away."

"What's the worst that could've happened?"

"Unthinkable pain, suffering, disgrace . . ."

"Chicken."

This is bad for our self-esteem. We have to think of a new idea.

The next plan, as much as I hate to own it, was all mine. I would test it out on a four-day solo hike on the AT near Bland, Virginia.

I was going to try to lose weight by packing only 4,000 calories. I figured that by walking a total of 50 miles, I would shed about a pound per day. I would report the results to Dave and impress him with my new dieting strategy. However, we had a long history of failed attempts at weight loss, so I was not surprised when he predicted that I would *gain* two pounds.

I went through my first day's calorie allotment well before suppertime, and though I had some hunger pangs, I slept well that night. The next day's 1,000 calories were devoured for breakfast. It would be a mighty long day of fat-burning.

That night at the shelter, the thru-hikers were eating big compared to me. I couldn't bring myself to bum food from them, so I dipped back into my food supply, not stopping until I had consumed all the next day's grub.

On the morning of the third day, I ate all of the final day's food. Even with those calories, I was weak and could barely move that day. I felt like my legs were eating themselves. That night I begged for food from thru-hikers—a new low. My plan was falling apart.

On the fourth morning, I was at my weakest point. Why wasn't my fat providing energy? I thought that was what fat cells did. I took a last look around for something to eat. No berries or wild onions along the trail. Still nothing in my empty food bag. After peering up and down the trail to make sure that no one was there to see me, I did the unimaginable. I reached into my pack and pulled out my container of Metamucil. A little extra fiber was sometimes important for me to be a happy hiker. However, I was about to take a half cup on an empty stomach. It was all I had left.

I drank about a quart of water so nothing would clog. True to an advertisement I once saw, you *do* need to chug your fiber. I was hungry enough that the orange flavor even tasted good that day. I guess it must have swelled up in my stomach because after waiting about twenty minutes or so and wondering what would happen I had the sensation of being completely full. It lasted an hour or two until I caught a ride to my car and finished the hike half a day early.

The next day Dave called. "Any luck?"

"I'll say!"

"Lose any?"

"Four pounds!" I bragged.

"I don't believe it. How?"

"Sorry. Gotta go!"

I have since learned that my body was metabolizing muscle tissue on that hike. Maybe brain cells, too. Obviously much-needed cells, judging by Dave's and my half-brained ideas.

MASSILLON SECTION

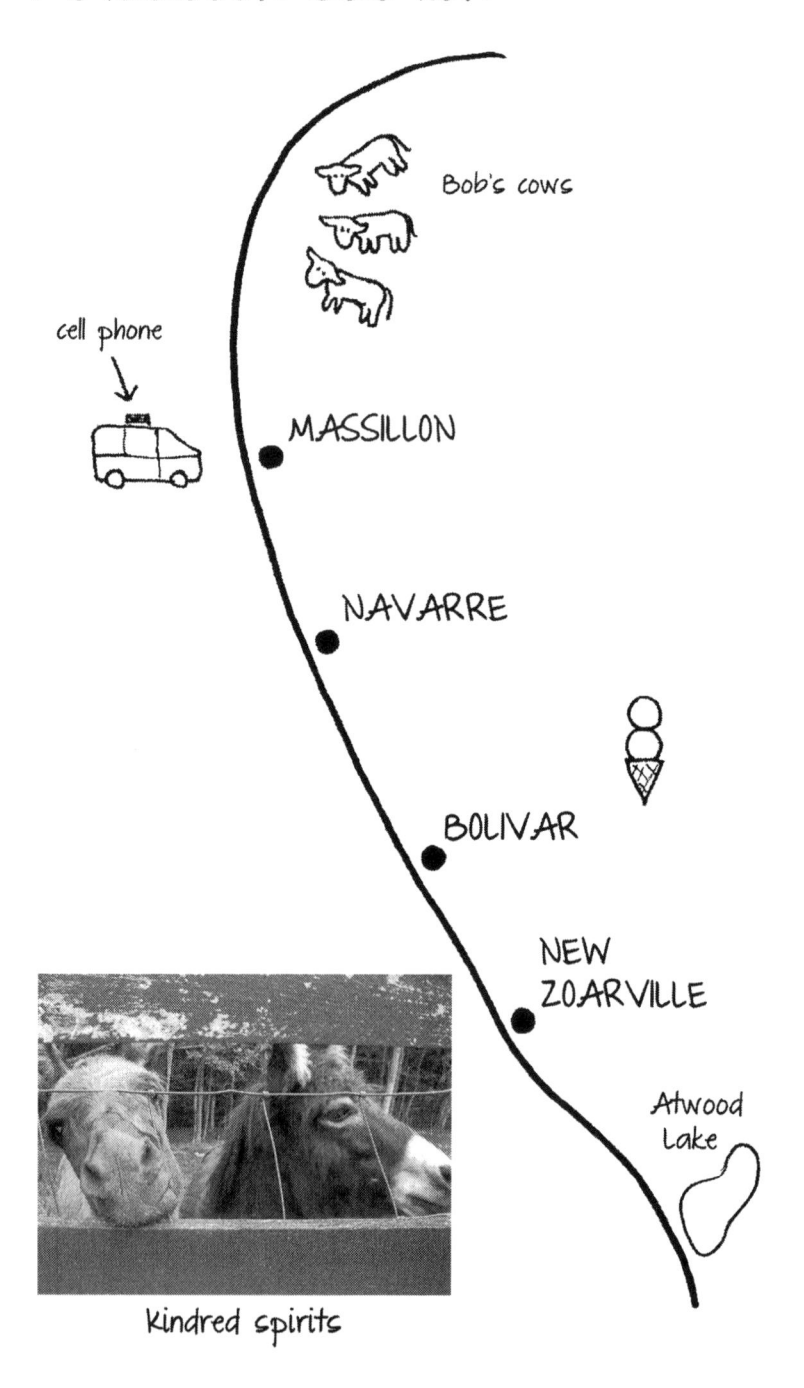

Bob's cows

cell phone

• MASSILLON

• NAVARRE

• BOLIVAR

• NEW ZOARVILLE

Atwood Lake

Kindred spirits

Journal Entry #11

Finding Kindred Spirits

Before I started hiking the Massillon section, I stopped in for a visit with Sis and her two giant Dobermans. You probably met her oldest, Booj. Rhymes with your nickname for me. Booj and Squooge are definitely kindred spirits. Booj loves me, and wouldn't let the newer dog, Butthead, anywhere near me.

I know how close you and Paula were. Given the reason I was hiking the BT, I invited Paula to join me on this section where the trail passed nearest to her house. She couldn't that weekend, but assured me that her heart (and of course my buddy Booj's) would go with me. She said if I could save a piece of the section for later, maybe she and "the boys" would walk it with me. She was still reeling from that Memorial Day. We had trouble even mentioning your name during my visit; it was just too early for a heart-to-heart talk about you.

When it was time to leave, Booj reluctantly gave me permission to hit the trail. I drove to a parking lot a mile north of Bolivar. As I hiked back through town, I stopped at the Dairy Queen before continuing south to New Zoarville. Since I was hiking alone, I had to keep retracing my steps back to the car and move it further down the trail. This gave me more time to enjoy the towpath. It also gave me a perfect excuse for a second stop at the DQ.

With 9 miles down and 45 left to go, I headed home.

◻ ◻ ◻

A few weeks later, I was able to return to this section with Bob. We hiked from New Zoarville to Atwood Lake. That leg took us into the foothills of the Appalachians with views of hills, farms, and lots of cows, horses, and other creatures. I snapped away because I can get Bonnie to look at my hiking pictures more enthusiastically if I include an ample number of critters in the bunch. Our favorites were two little donkeys. They went to Bob first. Must have been some good smelling food in his pack.

Seeing so many animals brought to mind John Trent and Gary Smalley's Personality Inventory. They have a method of classifying personality types by using four different animals. For example, a person who is a Lion (like our dad was) is strong-willed, decisive, and independent like his furry namesake. I took the test once and found that I was primarily a Golden Retriever. Quiet, dependable, diplomatic. I want things to be peaceful and for people to like me.

I would bet that Bob's dominant personality type is a Beaver. Lucky for me. Beavers are organizers, hard workers, and good planners. Bob meticulously plans each hike we do. He writes out step-by-step instructions for each day and gives me my own copy. Perfect. My job is to not lose it. He also takes detailed notes on all of our adventures and duplicates, by hand, a set for me. That's good because I never seem able to find my pencil. Sometimes I make Columbo look organized.

We hiked in another close-by section of the BT the following day, then returned home. Bob would use his Beaver skills again to plan our next hike, which would be in the northern half of the Massillon section.

◻ ◻ ◻

A few months passed before we made it back to finish the section. I checked in again with Paula to see if she could go with us, but Booj was sick and she couldn't leave him alone. She said to go ahead and asked if I would re-hike that piece with her sometime. *Absolutely. I don't want any trouble with Booj.*

On one of the three days, we started out in Massillon. We parked my car on a side street and walked south. I enjoyed being on the towpath trail again.

After a couple of miles I reached into my pocket for my cellphone but was unable to make a connection. I knew I hadn't put it in the pocket with the hole; I'd learned that lesson. (My Retriever tracking skills led me to recover my keys that time.) I hoped I had left my phone out of sight in the car, but I had this nagging feeling that I had left it *on* the car. I have had considerable experience with leaving cups of coffee and various other objects up there. Maybe I should install a cup holder and a locking glove box on my roof.

Bob offered to hike back to the car with me, but I opted to forge ahead. I had already hiked too many miles of this section twice. Besides, I still held out a little hope that the phone was in the car.

We reached Bob's car after walking almost twelve miles. When we arrived back at mine, my worst fears were confirmed: my phone was not inside. I was sure someone had grabbed it. I had TracFone disconnect my cell before the phone pirate started pranking the people in my phone directory. After all, the finder might be a fun-loving Otter.

We spent the other two days hiking up north of Massillon, partly on towpath trails, partly on back roads that brought us once again into Critterland.

At lunchtime one day, we found a great spot along a fence in the shade of a large mulberry tree and broke out our goodies. As soon as we sat down, 20 cows approached the other side of the barbed wire. (I know there were 20 because Bob counted them and recorded the number in his notes.) Just like the donkeys, they headed straight for Bob. Maybe they were partial to peanut butter and jelly. Or it could be that they just know a nice guy when they see one.

I've hiked much of the trail with Bob now. We've joked, prayed, argued, and persevered. I've learned some important lessons from him, one of them being that small gestures have a huge impact. He is always looking for simple ways to better a fellow hiker's day.

- Hold the limb for the person behind you so that it doesn't smack him silly.
- Pull up the barbed wire when someone is wiggling through a fence.
- Offer the end of your hiking stick to someone planted in a gulley.
- Share your PB&J with a friend who's run out of Beanie Weenies.

Talk about a great "sole" mate.

DAVE WAS DEFINITELY an Otter personality. Otters are outgoing, talkative, enthusiastic, and very often the life of the party. Crossing the Canadian border with Dave was always an adventure. It was another annual family fishing trip to Rice Lake, and Dave and I happened to be driving up together. This particular day Dave was trolling for a little trouble.

Agent: Citizenship?
Me: U.S.
Dave: Yes.
Agent: I mean *where*?
Dave: (Nodding his head in my direction) Same as him.

Agent: And that *iiiis . . . ?*

Dave: (Quickly turning to look at me) What was your answer, Squooge?

The agent looked behind us at the 57 cars in line, trying to decide what to do. I was surprised when he stayed with it a little longer.

Agent: What are you coming for?

Me: Fishing.

Dave: Because I have to.

Agent: Have to what?

Dave: Come with Squooge.

Agent: TO DO WHAT?

Dave: (Again looking at me with childlike innocence) What was your answer, Squooge?

You'd think we would have learned our lesson the last time we got pulled aside for a vehicle search. Obviously not. Another search this time proved that we were a little slow to learn that you don't play games at the border.

Another year, we neared the border about eleven o'clock at night. We still had several hours to drive to reach our cabin, so I implored Dave to bite his tongue. I reminded him that he owed me a huge favor for giving in and eating some of that muskie.

I was glad I had been coaching Dave ahead of time because when I pulled up to the line, two young agents with mischief in their eyes greeted us. It was almost as if they had expected us. Could it be that *they* would be the ones playing games at the border that day?

They asked, "State of residence?"

I answered, "Kentucky."

For some reason—I don't know why—the mischief in their eyes turned to great amusement when they heard where I lived. *Oh-oh, two more Otters.* Then they turned to my passenger and repeated, "State of residence?"

Dave looked at me with pleading eyes, but I stayed firm this time. "West Virginia," he choked.

Both guys burst into boisterous laughter. I could better understand the hilarity at Dave's response, but they still shouldn't have been making fun of my brother.

Lucky for the agents (and me) that it was late and Dave conceded that battle. They laughingly sent us on our way. We let them know what we thought, but only as we were traveling 100 kph on to our destination. Kentucky and West Virginia were firm allies for the night.

Though it is not one of Smalley and Trent's personality types, I guess everybody feels like a Donkey once in a while.

NORWALK SECTION

KA-BOOM!

TIFFIN

POLICE POLICE

WELLINGTON

A shady rest break for me courtesy of Poppie

Journal Entry #12

Finding Cover

Poppie, Bob, and I met at the western end of the Norwalk section after a long drive up. I'm sure Bonnie will be glad when I finish the BT so she can stop robbing other areas of our budget to feed the gasoline envelope. Gas isn't getting any cheaper.

The farmland there seemed conducive to getting in some serious mileage, so we planned on doing all 58.6 miles in three days. The flatness made me almost miss the hills that you and I loved to hate when we hiked, biked, or rode in your Jeep.

I heard distant explosions as we set off, but dismissed them for the time being. The wind that day was blustery and cold. Who was the "Jonah" who was responsible for all this turbulence? Who was running from God? It wasn't long before we found out, even without casting lots to do so. *Shame on you, Bob. Hiking on your wife's birthday.* Poppie and I decided not to throw him overboard, but definitely to keep an eye on him.

The first day's goal was 18.9 miles, even though Poppie thought we should have set it 3 to 5 miles higher. Poppie partly got his wish. Because of our intense political debates and failing to designate a blaze-watcher, we did put in an extra 4 miles—just not trail miles. When will we learn.

Ready for a good night's sleep at day's end, we drove to Tiffin and checked into the Tiffin Inn. The room was warm and clean and had a working shower; we were happy indoor campers. Bob had been boycotting Denny's for some reason, but since there was one sitting right at the end of the parking lot, he decided to give it another chance. For the rest of the hike Bob bragged up his chicken soup almost as much as he did his grandchildren. The hotcakes weren't too shabby either, so I ordered them again when we became repeat customers the next morning.

We left the restaurant and drove our vehicles to their predetermined locations. At first the stiff wind was annoying and uncomfortable, but after an hour or so the sun had transformed the day into one perfect for hiking the country roads. It also illuminated, for my floating eyeballs, a Port-A-John in the middle of nowhere. Was this my first trail mirage? I desperately hoped not. You are well aware that I am the "before" guy in the Flomax commercial. Mercifully, the vision turned out to be genuine. The john was the prized possession of a group of county construction workers replacing a washed-out bridge. Fortunately for me their mothers had taught them to share with others.

We talked a long time to one of the friendly crew members during his lunch break. One of the topics of conversation was Captain Blue. He is doing a thru-hike on the BT and had made quite an impression on those road workers. He had been through there just a week before (and was probably just as happy as I was to see the bathroom). From the beginning of his hike he said that he would keep going as long as it was fun, so I was glad to hear that he was still going. He is good publicity for the Buckeye Trail.

The events of the day took a strange turn when I picked up a bright yellow bucket from a ditch. Must have blown out of a road crew's truck. My foot was hurting, and the bucket made a good seat when I needed to rest. Each time I sat down, Poppie mockingly held my umbrella over my head.

I took a little heat from the guys for walking around carrying an umbrella under a blue sky. Before I hit 60 I would try to get as much sun as I possibly could. I recall you and me drifting around on a pontoon boat on Beech Fork Lake in Wayne County, you under the roof, me out on the sundeck trying to see how brown I could get. Now my Chrome Dome Umbrella reflects all those no-longer-wanted rays. Funny how things change.

Somebody in one of the farmhouses we passed must have noticed my newfound possession and figured that we were up to no good. I say that because shortly after noon a dark vehicle, and then another, pulled up behind us. Poppie kiddingly assumed the position up against the first car. The deputy, not joking, told us they had been investigating copper cable theft, cable associated with the search for petroleum. He said the explosions I heard the day before were probably part of that process.

While this conversation was going on, the second deputy was quietly standing behind his open door, window down and hands crossed just out of sight. Luckily, the interview went well for us; the police seemed satisfied that we were not carrying over a mile of cable in my bucket or in our packs. After recommending a place to eat, they told us about a historical plaque nearby that marked Military Road, a major supply route in the War of 1812.

The Huron County officers were professional and proficient, but at the same time they were polite. As they wished us a safe hike and got in their vehicles, we appreciated the fact that these guys would be watching out for us as we continued our 22-mile hike that day. We forged ahead to check out the centuries-old road.

No matter how fit I am or how flat the roads are, that distance is a long way to walk. Can you believe I'm doing this? I don't think we ever walked 22 miles together, at least not all in one day. But it beats sitting on the couch and thinking about our instant separation. Even out on the trail those thoughts often try to surface. That day they were making another disturbing appearance. It isn't like the times we got mad and didn't talk for weeks. We always knew we would get past them, and things might be even better. But this time no make-up call will be coming from either Kentucky or West Virginia.

The ill feelings swirling around in me about you, along with my close call with the law and the plantar fasciitis developing from walking across a chunk of the planet, had stirred up a foul mood in me. My companions were frazzled as well. Poppie's foot looked like hamburger. For the past two days he had been wrapping and rewrapping some ugly blisters acquired on an earlier hike. Bob had some relentless hip pain. He was trying to finish the BT before possibly getting a joint replacement. We all needed some sleep so that we wouldn't strangle each other.

Apparently we had come to the wrong place to get any shuteye. We had reserved a little cabin in a campground that was not officially open yet for the season. Bob's bed curled like a banana. Poppie's mattress had holes from which hungry varmints likely peered, just waiting for him to fall asleep so they could nibble on his toes. I was the only one small enough to use the ladder up to the loft and was relieved that my mattress seemed normal. Although I felt a little guilty for getting the best bed, I unrolled my sleeping bag on top of it and tried to put the day behind me.

All night long I heard stirring and groaning from below. Daylight found Bob sorer than the day before and Poppie out in his car trying to get some sleep. Poppie finally hobbled in and told us that he would have to bail (even after I offered to share my bucket). We understood; we were surprised his toe was still attached. Those blisters were worse than any I've ever had, and maybe as bad as that disgusting one you developed on your baby toe on the AT.

With the beginning of a new day, I wasn't feeling as rotten about you as I was the day before—just so you know. My feelings about you change like the weather. The saying goes that if you don't like the weather, just wait a few minutes. On this hike I am learning that just because one day I have painful memories that I don't think I can bear doesn't mean that the next day won't bring pleasant memories of our times together.

The weather conditions that day were constant rain and temperatures in the low 40s. Bob and I decided to make it easier on ourselves while doing those last 18 miles. It had dawned on us that we could space the cars only 5 or 6 miles apart that day. That gave us more chances to dry out and rest while we leapfrogged the vehicles, and it offered more opportunities to drive to a bathroom if necessary. We liked this method so much that we plan to practice it in the future whenever we can.

During one of our shuttles, we stopped at the Subway in Wellington. When the Subway staff heard that we were out hiking on that rainy, miserable day, they served us at our table. Along with our subs, they brought us some broken, but warm and fresh (and free), cookies. Our bodies were revived; we would be able to finish the last five miles.

The rain picked up, and I razzed Bob as he broke out, of all things, a big umbrella to complement my Chrome Dome. A thoughtful lady stopped to offer us a ride. We politely declined, but warned her against picking up weirdos like us in the future. She appeared to appreciate the humor.

When we saw the Rochester First Baptist Church in the distance, we knew we were close to finding cover in Bob's Journey. Sometimes my umbrella was just not enough. But then, sometimes neither was a vehicle . . .

DAVE'S FIRST VEHICLE WAS A JEEP. For its inaugural run, we headed to Daniel Boone National Forest in Kentucky for a three-day adventure over a Fourth of July weekend. We had both seen a lot of Jeep commercials, and we fantasized about being in an ad of our own.

On the day we arrived, we just rode around looking cool. Too bad so few people were on those back roads in the forest to see us. This continued into day two until we found a trace of a road turning off of a gravel road and decided to explore it. We were both surprised at the steepness of the whoop-de-doos we encountered, but Dave's Jeep had no trouble negotiating them.

The weather forecaster had not seen any rain in his crystal ball for our trip, so Dave had left the top of his Jeep at home. That began to seem like a bad idea when a passing bramble nailed me. And it seemed like an even worse idea when we passed what I thought was a still.

I began to consider that we just might be trespassing, and that we had picked a lousy place to do it. I couldn't remember any of the commercials offering advice to Jeep customers who happened into this type of situation. I suggested that we do a u-ey, hoping desperately that Dave would cooperate, but he was having too much fun charging ahead to oblige me. I was not a happy Jeeper when he suggested adding moonshine to our tank to assist in a speedier getaway.

These were typical behaviors for Dave and me. He liked to cross boundary lines so he would know where they were, and then back up just short of them. I tend to stay away from where I think the boundary is. Maybe a bit unexciting, but at least safe.

Even though it was like navigating a maze, we eventually made it back to the gravel road, and finally to asphalt. We didn't want to be late for the feature movie nearby at the drive-in. A war flick was playing, so we loaded up on rations in the snack building and settled into our vehicle for a night of adventure—hopefully to be experienced more vicariously than our afternoon's escapade.

Soon after the movie started, and while the snacks were being greedily consumed, the battle on the screen escalated until it sounded like an Independence Day celebration. As we imagined our Wrangler dodging missiles and rockets like its ancestors did in The Big One, bottle rockets began to burst against the screen. How cool was that! It added a great 3-D effect to the movie, with no special glasses needed.

However, the high-fives ended as quickly as they had started when a bottle rocket exploded ten feet above our heads. A second blast sent us both diving under the Jeep.

As we cowered prostrate on the ground, I could see in Dave's wide-eyed expression that he had finally had his fill of adventure. It didn't take us long to come to a joint decision: the next time we went there on a Fourth of July weekend we would have a top on our vehicle, or at least wear helmets and flak jackets.

Even day three was memorable. Driving 150 miles home in the rain in a topless Jeep while wearing unfashionable garbage-bag ponchos is hard to forget.

In retrospect, maybe with a cover on the Jeep I wouldn't have experienced one of the best weekends Dave and I spent together—better than anything the commercials could offer.

MOGADORE SECTION

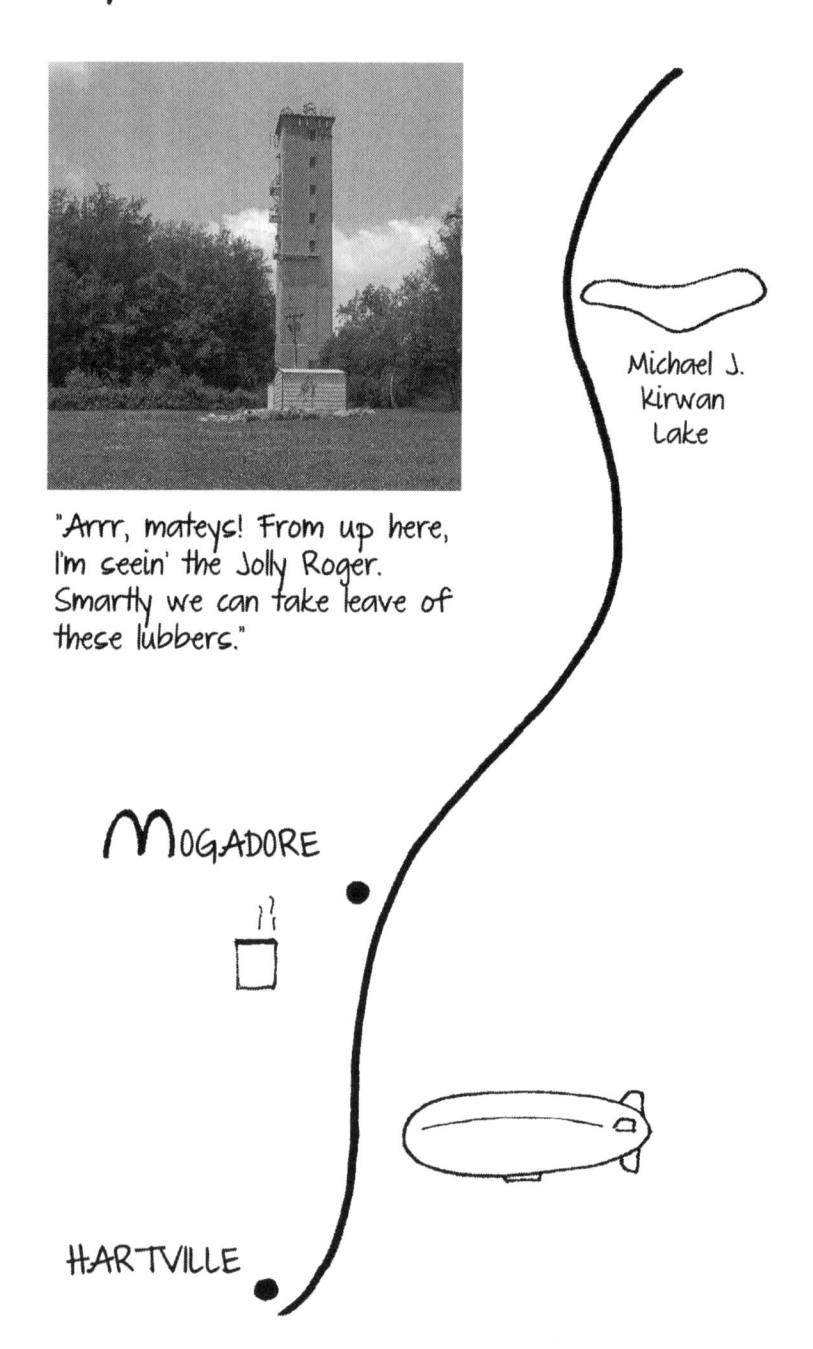

"Arrr, mateys! From up here, I'm seein' the Jolly Roger. Smartly we can take leave of these lubbers."

Michael J. Kirwan Lake

MOGADORE

HARTVILLE

Journal Entry #13

Finding Nourishment for Body and Soul

Bob and I planned to conquer most of the Mogadore section in one trip north. As we often did, we rendezvoused at McDonald's. I always enjoy starting my hikes at the golden arches rather than the blue blazes. I love filling up on their tasty brew—even though it causes me problems when it expires miles from any restroom. But any negative consequences that I am forced to deal with are usually balanced by the pleasant childhood memories that come to mind as I sit under the arches drinking coffee with my hiking buddies.

You wouldn't share this particular memory, Dave, but over half a century ago I sat behind a counter at Jefferson Diner beside my best friend, Dad, listening to "I'm Sorry" playing on the jukebox, drinking an "adult beverage" with him, and feeling special. We would then go off to work. Dad would cut brush for the family sawmill business and I tagged along to cover his back. He sprayed kerosene on the small stumps that remained. To this day, that pungent smell takes me right back into those deep woods with Dad. I wonder what Dad did to make *you* feel important when he went from tending saws to tending souls.

You and I could have done a lot of reminiscing about our younger days if we could have walked together along the country roads and through the well-maintained parks in this section. The sounds, smells, and sights had a way of bringing those days back to my memory. I could have even shown you the ins and outs of cutting brush.

The section is named after a small town nestled in its center. The name Mogadore was imported from a village in Morocco, adopted during an era of pillaging pirates and wandering nomadic hordes. No seas or deserts in sight, but you probably would have conjured up some adventure. You always did have a rich imagination, and you were constantly trying to get me to play along.

I can easily envision you wearing an eye patch and a hook, and sporting a parrot on your shoulder. The peak of a tall tower we passed would have provided an excellent view of the surrounding countryside. With your spyglass you might have spotted a distant skull and crossbones. There was never a dull moment when you were around.

Not only did you have a healthy imagination, but you also had quite an appetite. I still have one; the guys I hike with will attest to that. You and I always figured we'd lose weight when we hiked, and I had hopes that this 50-mile trek with Bob would carve off a pound or two. However, the first night of the hike we stayed at Bob's condo in Boardman where his wife Sissy tried to fatten us up with barbequed chicken, potatoes, and ice cream. I found my hopes losing muscle.

Day two found us hiking by Michael J. Kirwan Lake in West Branch State Park, named after an Ohio congressman who tried for decades to get a canal built from Lake Erie to Pittsburgh. The Pirates could have sailed from the Great Lakes straight to PNC Park if he had been successful. Jokers called it "Kirwan's Big Ditch." I say, give the late Congressman a little credit. I admire people who never stop trying.

Things were going fine until a trail gremlin (probably a twig) reached up from the path and tripped me. I hit the ground so hard I felt obligated to apologize. I was disoriented and sore all over as Bob helped me to my feet. He kept a close eye on me throughout the rest of the hike to make sure I was OK.

That night Bob returned to his condo and I drove up to Dorset to visit Aunt Mary and Uncle Jim. Since I would be arriving past suppertime and didn't expect to be fed, I picked up a loaded pizza in Jefferson to take with me. Jefferson Diner was closed when I passed it, but I made a mental note to stop in someday and drop some coins in the jukebox.

When I arrived in Dorset, Aunt Mary had barbequed ribs, corn, mashed potatoes and gravy, and apple pie waiting for me. I should have known better than to think she wouldn't have a feast ready. To avoid cramps, we waited an hour before we dug into the pizza. Any hope of losing weight this hike was getting slimmer.

We spent two more days finishing the trail. We got lost twice, but there were no more injuries. On a back road, we did happen upon a large dog that looked as though it had had more than its share of troubles. Two people were trying to help it, but it wouldn't let anyone near. We could hear its low growl—not vicious, but one that revealed a lot of distress and discomfort. Bob and I offered it some hiker cuisine by gently laying the food on the road as close as it would allow us. Eventually hunger got the best of our new friend, but then it went back into the edge of the woods. We felt a little better when one of the Good Samaritans said she would return with her husband; they had rescued other dogs along that road.

As we walked on, we noticed the Goodyear Blimp drifting overhead. Its shadow was not that much bigger than mine at this stage of the hike. And mine was to grow even bigger when we reached the chocolate shop in Hartville, and later that evening when we ate spaghetti at Bob's condo. My neck still ached from my earlier fall as I gazed upward at the supersized airship, but I was thankful that at least everything still worked.

It also helped that Bob cared. It's healthy for the soul to have friends like him. And it was just plain fun for my taste buds that the chocolate shipment had gotten past the pirates and into Hartville.

THE POTATOES WE REQUESTED—no longer buried down on the farm, but now under swarms of steamy homemade noodles and gravy—were accompanied by endless buttery biscuits and slices of chewy banana bread, washed down with scalding coffee, and followed, as usual, by raspberry cobbler and two scoops of ice cream.

This is how Dave and I prepared for our workouts: careful stretching of our stomach muscles, warming up our coffee cups, and finally, pushing up from the table. Now we could safely exercise off our lunch. Maybe later we could start on those calories from breakfast that were already getting too comfortable. If our comfort food diet plan had worked, Dave and I could have made a fortune partnering with Bob Evans. It hadn't so far, but that never stopped us from giving it another wholehearted try.

We began our bike ride in Ritter Park where we pedaled the easier paths before moving out to the hills around Huntington. Carbohydrate loading was not working for me, but in an hour Dave let me catch up, offering to trade his mount for mine. I declined and took off again, luckily downhill at first. However, after more hills and another hour had passed, I was ready to swap.

As Dave acquainted himself with the intricacies of my Huffy, I darted off ahead. With a big grin I turned to wave good-bye with one hand, my other still gripping the handlebar. When I turned back around, a stop sign had jumped out in front of me.

Apparently, Italian designer bikes have extremely sensitive brakes. That was certainly true of the one I used that grabbed the front rim. I obeyed the sign, as well as the law of gravity. After I flew over the handlebars, I landed on the concrete with a painful bounce or two. Then the bike flew over me and did its own bouncing.

Sometimes it is just impossible not to look as dumb as you feel. I hoped no one had a camera—at least one with film in it. For an instant I wished I had been injured more severely than only the cuts and bruises I had suffered, just so I could get some sympathy. But it wasn't necessary. Dave approached, brakes squeaking, and proceeded to apply first aid to my hurt pride. He wasn't worried right then about his bike—just his brother.

That ended the day's exercise. We got back to the truck and headed for the DQ. The day turned out to be a net gain all around for me. A big yes for accumulating calories, but also for learning that my pride trumped Dave's expensive ride. Kinda makes a brother feel special.

Part Two

Losing Direction

BOWERSTON SECTION

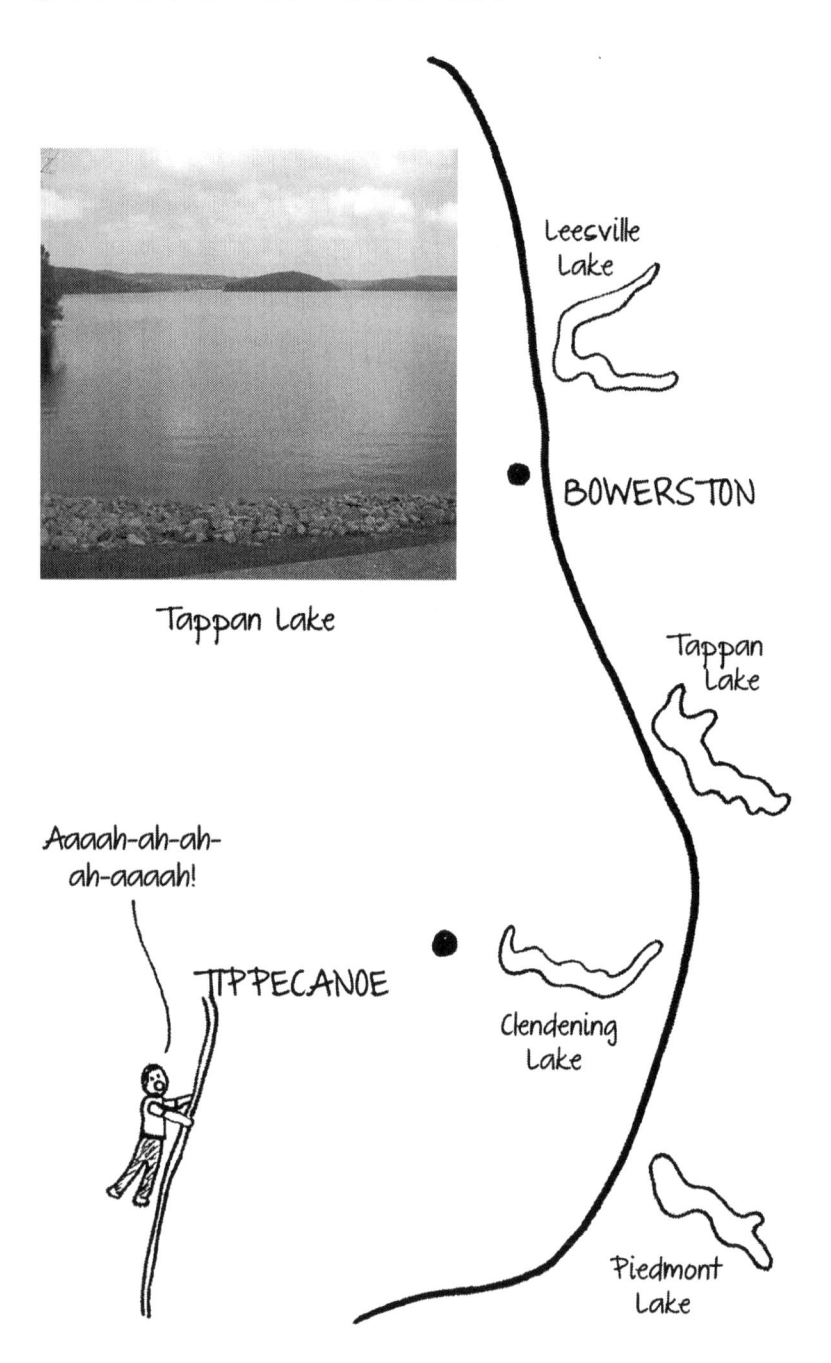

Tappan Lake

Leesville Lake

● BOWERSTON

Tappan Lake

Aaaah-ah-ah-ah-aaaah!

TIPPECANOE

Clendening Lake

Piedmont Lake

Journal Entry #14

Remembering Some Valleys

Once again I was transported back to my school days, this time via the Bowerston section. Each day, we hiked 12 to 13 miles of hilly terrain while Bob's listening ear downloaded stories from my childhood, many formed right there in the hills of the Muskingum Watershed Conservancy District.

Even though that area does not boast the highest altitude on the BT (it's up at Hinckley Reservation in the Medina section), the height of the hills is exaggerated by the deep river valleys of the region. Those valleys are being kept in check by dams built in the '30s by the MWCD. The dams hold back Leesville, Tappan, Clendening, and Piedmont Lakes in this section. The BT skirts all of them.

It's amazing—those hills seem only half as high now as they did when I was a child, yet they are twice as hard to climb. Clendening Lake still sparkles like a massive gem, but now I'd rather chill out on its banks than in its nippy waters. Nevertheless, those hills and corresponding valleys strike a chord in my soul and bring back those magical times when we lived in Tippecanoe.

Your playpen sat in the parsonage, or out in the yard if you were lucky, but my daily habitat was in the woodlands surrounding town. Dad let me run the hills. However, if he had known that my friends and I were training to be stuntmen for Tarzan, swinging on grapevines over deep gorges, he probably would have grounded me from those woods to this day. No doubt you were busy figuring out ways to escape from your pen and have some adventures of your own.

While Bob and I navigated the high hills above Clendening, I told him about the trip I had made there in 2004. I don't know if I ever told you about that one.

□ □ □

I had just received a copy of *Follow the Blue Blazes*. After looking at the table of contents, I rifled through the pages to find the Lake Country chapter. One of the featured hikes was on the Clendening! I excitedly prepared for my trip, promising Bonnie I would dial down the adventure a notch from my childhood years. She said, "Yeah, right," and I took off.

As I passed through the "metropolis" of Tippecanoe, I noticed that it hadn't changed much in the half century since we lived there: still no stoplights, restaurants, or subdivisions. That is one of the things I love about this area. It is refreshing to see that urban sprawl is not universal.

The hike was 12 miles long, and I had decided to take two days. I hoped (I think) to see one of the bobcats or bears Mr. Pond indicated in his book as being inhabitants of this area. Clendening Lake is the largest undeveloped lake in Ohio, and if I were a bobcat or a bear, I would choose to live in those woods and try to be occasionally sighted by hikers.

On day one I topped a large hill. I was concentrating on the trail and still trying to catch my breath when a huge shadow engulfed me. It was too big to be cast by a bobcat, or even a bear. I slowly raised my head and discovered its source. Flashing before me were the eyes of an enormous bull.

We both froze for a few very long seconds, staring each other down—one of us emanating fear, the other exuding fearlessness. (Guess which one I was.) The bull moved first, making a fake charge. I think he took only a step or two toward me, but I didn't have time to count. I found that you *can* move quickly while wearing a heavy backpack. I'm sure I could have even climbed a tree with it if he had kept coming.

I had passed a hiker a mile or so back, so at a safe distance from the bull, I waited for my new best friend to catch up. We figured we would each have a 50 percent chance of outrunning the bull. When we topped the hill, he was 20 feet off the trail; so was a herd of cows. I was sure he was smirking at me as we passed.

□ □ □

As Bob and I approached the same hill, I was almost hoping for a return engagement. I wanted proof so he would believe my bull story. However, no bovines were present, and he was probably thinking, "Yeah, right." Bulls would just have to be added to the list of "occasionally sighted" creatures on the BT. Kind of like it was between you and me in the late '90s.

DAVE WAS A HOMEBODY, preferring to entertain me in Wayne County rather than travel to my house. Trips away from home were a big deal for him, so I felt special when he said he was coming to see Bonnie and me for what was intended to be a three-day visit. He loaded up his gas-guzzling New Yorker and headed for Kentucky.

When Dave did take a vacation, it was important that it was carefully planned, and especially that it was thoroughly enjoyed. I spent most of the first day with him, except for a few hours that I had to work. Among other places, we went to one of the overlooks in Eden Park in Cincinnati. We enjoyed the view of the Ohio River dotted with barges and a variety of watercraft. I thought it was cool that we got to share this together since we had never managed to get to Chimney Top Rock at the same time.

That evening came the planning for day two. I explained to Dave that Bonnie or I would be available for all but a few hours. The thought never occurred to me that it wouldn't be OK with him.

When I got up the next morning, I noticed that his car was not in the driveway. *Probably another trip to the gas station.* A little later I noticed that Dave's bag was gone as well. I knew then that the land yacht had set sail for home. Apparently, Dave was not into "staycations" when it meant staying with his brother.

He probably thought that I wasn't taking this vacation thing seriously enough. There might have been some truth in that. On the other hand, Dave was single and carefree at the time. He might not have understood why I couldn't skip all of my work responsibilities for the day to hang out with him. Or perhaps our river-watching had reminded him of the stream flowing by his house and he was being drawn back home. I never did find out the reason for his unexpected departure.

Weeks passed with no contact between us. I'm not sure why. Maybe it was to see who would call first. We both had a good dose of the Spencer stubborn gene. The weeks turned into months, then into more than a year.

At times it took a lot of work for Dave and me to get along. Sometimes we enjoyed a close relationship, but at other times it was as if some subtle, almost mysterious, battle was going on. So many real, and probably some imagined, gripes existed between us that it must have seemed easier at the time to expend our energies on anything other than our relationship. The late '90s found us both busier than normal. Dave was getting Wayne County ready for Y2K, and I was getting involved in more and more extracurricular activities with students and parents at school.

Sometimes I felt optimistic and thought that we would get through this deep valley and enter the new millennium with a restored relationship. Other times I thought, *Yeah, right.*

SHAWNEE SECTION

Jet engine testing facility

Me, Charles, Jim, John, and Bob at Shawnee Lodge

Shawnee Lodge

Day Hike Trail

Journal Entry #15

Finding Common Ground

I set out on Ohio Pike again for yet another trek in the Shawnee section. It was trip number four, but who was counting. That day's hike would complete the Shawnee segment of my BT journey.

I would be hiking with Bob and his friend Andy, making a total of eight people I'd shared this section of the trail with. I know this would shock you. Neither of us was exactly a social butterfly. In fact, I'm still trying to work my way up to social pupa. I had been in no hurry to finish this section, and I didn't mind the drive at all.

I love Ohio's "Little Smokies": as much for the memories you and I shared there as for its misty mountains; as much for the new friends I made there as for some new flora and fauna I encountered.

Speaking of fauna, I honked back at the flock of geese that flew overhead and hoped that they were smart enough to stay away from jet engines. No big airports are in the area, but up ahead close to my destination, testing to make aircraft engines as safe as possible was going on at the Peebles GE jet engine testing facility.

□ □ □

My first hike in the Shawnee section took place several months ago. It began near that facility. Charles, a fellow hiker, was a GE employee who got us cleared to take a three-hour tour. Not just anyone could have gotten in there.

I don't know exactly what I'm allowed to tell you, but I suppose they wouldn't have shown us anything that was top secret. You should have seen the test they did to make sure the engines they produce are goose-proof. The birds are shot from a special type of cannon into an operating engine. Not to worry, though. We were assured that all the birds had accidentally met their demise before they arrived at the facility.

Following the tour, we broke for lunch. Still replaying the geese getting cooked, I didn't eat as much as usual. Nevertheless, even with a rather empty stomach, I enjoyed the wonderful seven-mile hike. I don't need to explain to you the beauty of those hills since you and I roamed them quite frequently. You'd also understand how their ruggedness helped me regain my appetite in time for the next test: how much catfish I could eat at Shawnee Lodge that evening.

After camping that night at the state park, we met at the gate in the morning for hot drinks and donuts. Shawnee State Park's Annual Fall Hike was taking place that day. Our group represented the Buckeye Trail Association. A good piece of the day's featured hike was on the Buckeye Trail, so I got in seven more miles.

We enjoyed cider straight from an apple press set up along the trail for the day's festivities. To end the day, the Friends of Shawnee State Park treated everyone to bean soup cooked in a huge iron kettle, with tasty chunks of cornbread to sop it up.

Though it had been another day without major mileage, it was one with major memories. BTA members come from many different walks of life, but for that day, we walked the same path. It's fun meeting all kinds of people: blue and white collar, young and old, experienced and occasional hikers, much like the variety of folks you hosted in your back yard in West Virginia. As part of my social metamorphosis program, I at least said hi and introduced myself to every new face I saw.

On the other two trips to that section, I hiked with Jim, Bob, and some of Bob's friends. We got in some serious miles. I especially liked passing through a tiny portion of the 8,000-acre wilderness area of the Shawnee State Forest where timber cutting and motorized vehicles aren't allowed. It was pretty cool looking out towards the Ohio River from there, the hills covered with the bluish haze produced by the moisture the forest emits.

I tried to imagine the Shawnee standing in the same spot four hundred years ago, loving this area, only to be driven out by the Iroquois. They came back and I can understand why. You and I returned there often to enjoy its beauty. After they returned, they were forced to leave again, this time by the treaties of the white settlers. As vast as the region was, it wasn't big enough to allow both societies to coexist peacefully.

□ □ □

Twenty miles later the geese were far behind me, but not the recollections of our adventures in Shawnee. Each mile I drove on that final trip to complete the section seemed to bring back more memories, many of which expressed themselves through my tear ducts. But driving *toward* the pain always seemed to lessen its intensity.

I "accidentally" passed up the parking lot where I was to meet Bob and Andy. Instead, I drove to the trailhead of the Day Hike Trail. I pulled into the spot where I had parked so many times in the past, but this time your van was missing. Darn sun was making my eyes water again. When I finally pulled myself together, I headed back to the main parking lot. Andy and Bob were there waiting.

SOMETIME AFTER Y2K, birthday calls—a tradition going back many years—resumed between Dave and me. This was the gateway for occasional e-mails, which eventually led to non-birthday calls that began with probing questions like "What's up?" and "How 'bout those Bengals?" This may not sound like much, but for us, at least at the time, it was heavy stuff.

One day we came up with the idea of hiking together again. That was one bridge between us that was still sturdy enough to venture across. As with many of our activities, our new idea was based on total spontaneity. It was somewhat like our Meet Me at the Rock game, but with no loser. We were never sure when the "HIKE?" subject line would pop up on our e-mails—but we would make every effort to answer "YES! WHEN?" when one did appear. Other things could wait. Somehow we knew that these get-togethers could not.

When we agreed on a time, I would go through my usual pre-hike ritual:
- Make the dreaded weather check.
- Cancel, postpone, reschedule, or just ignore other stuff.
- Toss my most up-to-date low-tech gear into the car.
- Double-check my stash of chocolate and ibuprofen.
- Motor towards Shawnee State Park.

Shawnee was strategically located between our homes. We would meet at the trailhead of the Day Hike Trail. The 7.2-mile loop had everything we loved: fresh air, steep hills, and scenic vistas. We didn't state any lofty goals, other than making it to the tops of the hills ahead of us, but I think we wanted to get more in sync with each other as much as we wanted a physical workout.

Some days it was 7.2 miles of mostly quiet walking, the silence acceptable to both of us as we concentrated on getting our footing and our next breath. During those times, I didn't feel as if I had to fill every sound void with words. We were content to listen to the breeze stirring the sleepy leaves, a flock of geese honking as they flew overhead, or an occasional "jet" that never appeared over the horizon.

Other days one or both of us would have a lot to say, barely getting it all said in 7.2 miles. We could spend the entire day planning our big hike on the AT. Or we would discuss our books and our bikes.

Though we tried to keep our conversations lighthearted, now and then a serious topic would crop up. Our family had its share of stuffy relational issues that needed to be brought into the open and aired out. Serious talks could stir up old conflicts. When that happened, we would try to resolve our differences before we got back to the parking lot. On a good day we were successful, even if we only agreed to disagree. Then we could enjoy each other's companionship for the rest of the hike. When we couldn't get past our discord, it seemed as if we would never reach the lot.

At times it seemed a little silly to drive 85 miles to hike such a relatively short distance. I can't really say what grudges got settled or how our communication improved. But I do know that those hills, though they hadn't seen the Shawnee and the settlers come together a few centuries before, now witnessed brothers becoming friends.

All in 7.2 really good miles.

BEDFORD SECTION

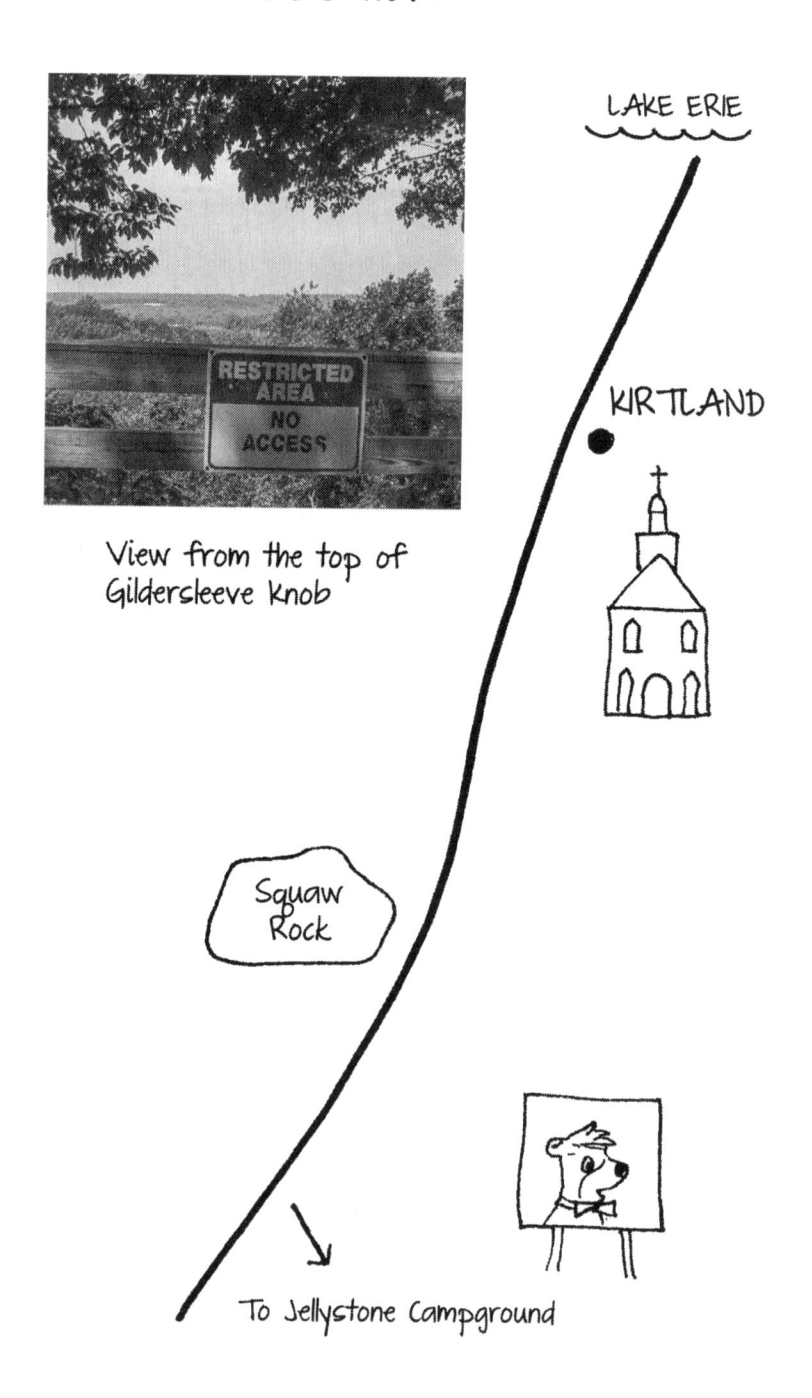

View from the top of Gildersleeve knob

LAKE ERIE

KIRTLAND

Squaw Rock

To Jellystone Campground

Journal Entry #16

Finding the Message

Dad became a minister when I was 10, so I spent the next eight years in pews. You spent *all* of your at-home years in church, unless Dad let you opt out in high school, which seems about as likely as a church pot-luck supper with no green beans or scalloped potatoes.

I can't recall us discussing religion much. I do know that we were PKs with different views of Christianity. You were sometimes skeptical of other church people's behavior, and not always without good reason; I was more tolerant of our shortcomings, believing we are works in progress.

One statement you made on that Memorial Day weekend when we were discussing our beliefs puzzled me: you said I needed to "step out there." It didn't seem to fit into the context of our conversation. Like so many other things you said that weekend, I couldn't fully grasp what you were trying to tell me. Finally, out of frustration, I tried to write off your directive as an admonition for me to be more open-minded. Even then, those words continued to trouble me.

Bob and I found something just as mysterious along the BT. On our second day of hiking in the Bedford section, we came near Squaw Rock. The famous landmark was not far from the trail, sitting alongside the Chagrin River. My foot was hurting, so while I nursed it and looked at photos of the rock on a brochure, Bob went down the hill to investigate.

The sandstone bears the images of, among other things, a woman, a quiver of arrows, an eagle, a giant serpent and a papoose. Additional images of ships, a frontiersman, a log cabin, and Washington D.C.'s original capital building are found on the river face of the rock. Many think the sculpture conveys the mistreatment of Native Americans, some, a history of the country, but no one knows for sure.

Like thousands before him, Bob pondered the message that Henry Church had tried to communicate on the rock in the late 1800s. Being the intuitive man that Bob is, I was sure he would get it. But it was to remain a mystery. I would have liked to see if he could decipher your "step out there" message—but I wasn't ready to share that one.

All that pondering can make a person hungry. I couldn't wait to get back to Jellystone Campground for a second night's stay. My plan included watching old cartoons on an outdoor screen while eating a PB&J that I had yogied from Bob. A good night's sleep inspired one more day of hiking in the woods, after which we returned home.

Even though my foot was still hurting, we returned a couple of weeks later to try to finish the section. When my foot got good and sore, we decided to step off the BT and take a short drive to visit the city of Kirtland. We wanted to see the first temple built by Joseph Smith and his followers. The problem for Joseph and the rest of the Mormons in 1836, the year the temple was dedicated, was that some people *didn't* want to see it—or see the people who worshipped differently. Within a few years, the majority of the Mormons had moved farther west.

The religious differences you and I had could have driven *us* apart, but we usually tried to keep our beliefs below the radar when we were together. I'm glad we had decided that our differing views on God, as well as some other touchy topics, were not going to sink us.

Later that day, we were back on the trail. Exiting the "Emerald Necklace," the beautiful string of connected parks circling Cleveland, we entered Chapin Forest. I limped to the top of Gildersleeve Knob, which is an impressive 1,160 feet above sea level. A sign warned people away from the Sharon Conglomerate Ledges for the protection of the vegetation, and probably for the safety of people like Bob and me as well.

From our vantage point on the Glaciated Allegheny Plateau, we could see the lake plain in the distance. A careful observer might be able to see Lake Erie 8 miles away, or even Cleveland at 18 miles, but it was too hazy that day for us to get that mileage.

The Lake Erie Plain and the Allegheny Plateau have something in common: they were both formed by glaciers. But they each have distinct features as well, which can make for some disturbing weather. As the moisture-laden air from Lake Erie passes over the plateau in the winter, the snow flies.

Just like it did between you and me sometimes.

DAVE WOULD HARDLY EVER come out and just give me the bottom line. I knew instinctively that it was my role to discover it myself. Like that note taped to his refrigerator door. On official-looking paper, he had printed off the words "SQUOOGE-FREE ZONE." I have never figured that one out. It wasn't that I was being denied access to the food inside, considering the many times that I reached in and snagged a snack with no consequences (at least from Dave). I questioned him a time or two about the note, but I wasn't able to gain any new insights.

One day Dave was piloting his giant land yacht. We were driving the back roads in Daniel Boone Forest, and Dave was talking about various types of damage that crashes could inflict on an auto. I wondered why the sudden interest. I couldn't see anything damaging that cruiser.

Miles passed, but the subject didn't. Dave started honing in on windshields. He remarked that he was beginning to see fewer and fewer shattered windshields on wrecked vehicles that were being towed from crash sites. Fewer *redstained* shattered windshields. It finally clicked—my seat belt, that is. All of that, instead of "buckle up" when I slid into the passenger seat. *Good one, Dave.*

Years later, we were riding bikes along the Greenbrier River in West Virginia and we pulled into a small town. My Huffy seat had been giving me a little problem, so Dave directed me to the town's bike shop. He knew the owner and told her his big brother was having issues. The solution turned out to be bike shorts that cost me more than I had paid for my bike. However, as we pedaled away, I found that I was pleased with my pricey new discovery. I was able to sit on the seat again without wincing. I figured that now I just might be able to handle the 25-mile ride back to the cabin.

We carried on a conversation above the tune that the tires were playing on the gravel path. We discussed how the world had changed since we were kids, how you just couldn't trust people like in the good old days. Now you had to look people over a lot more carefully.

As we cycled on, the conversation geared up a bit. Dave began talking about suspicious looking characters: characters sporting dark glasses, characters keeping their heads down . . . *characters wearing speedos.* I finally got it. I did look scary in them. (At least I wasn't riding my Stalker.) Dave hinted that they should work just as well, and create less attention, if I put my cut-offs back on over them. I took the hint. The good people in the neighborhoods we were riding by could rest easy once more.

In the fall of 2007, Dave became insistent on spending time with our relatives in Ashtabula County. For the past few years he had only seen them at funerals. Even though there was an early snowfall and Dave didn't like to drive in the snow, he was set on making the trip. Since we were each traveling from our own homes, we drove north separately to see our cousin Donnie, Aunt Mary, and Uncle Jim.

What a visit it was. After a meal of ribs, potatoes, and corn on the cob, we said yes to apple pie and ice cream as well. Dave was center stage and at his best. He had done a stint as a stand-up comic out West during his younger years, and we all could understand why. He had a line a minute. He also had a ready-made audience who appreciated his humor.

We reminisced about childhood, especially the times we spent down the road at Grandpa's house. Seems as though there were always a couple of cousins there to play with. We reluctantly retired at a late hour. Dave had work to do in the morning before we could leave for home.

Donnie's and Aunt Mary's computers had been giving them fits. We all knew Dave was the man for the job. After fixing Aunt Mary's computer, Dave spent considerable time working on Donnie's. I heard him sing a silly little four-line ditty into the mic. I wondered what that was all about, but I didn't give it too much thought at the time. Sometimes I forgot that Dave was always working on getting a message across, even though it was often in cryptic form.

When Dave completed his work, we said our goodbyes and returned home. For the time being, the mystery of the silly song would remain in the Squooge-free Zone.

ROAD FORK SECTION

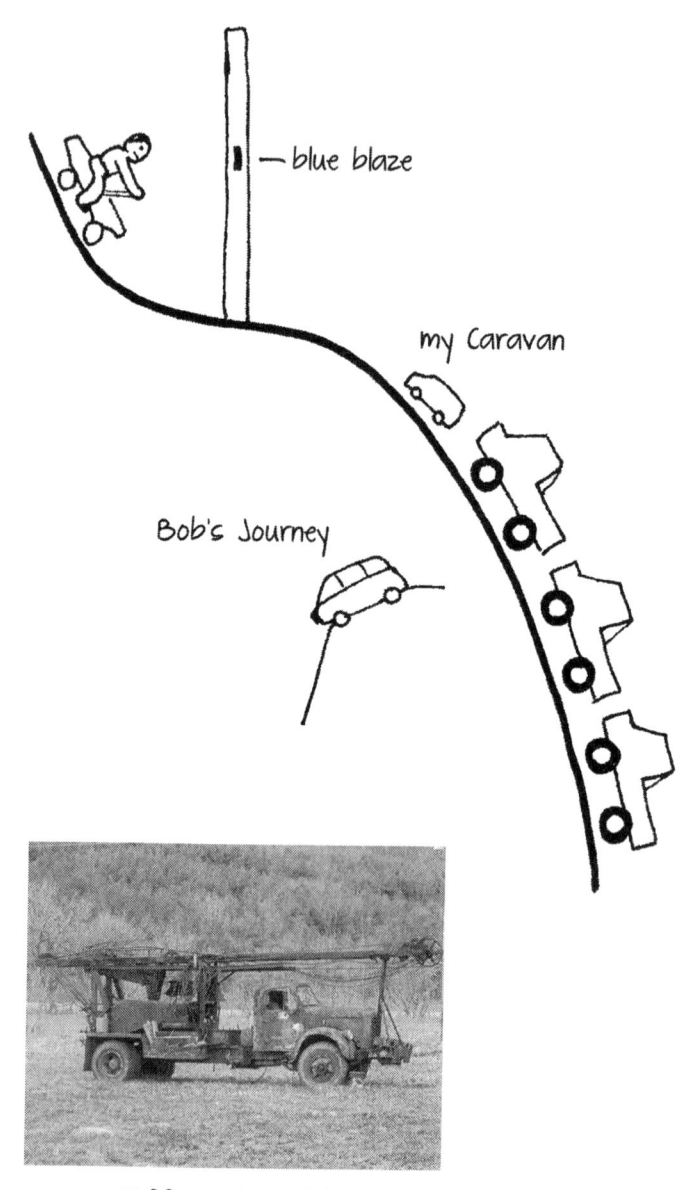

blue blaze

my Caravan

Bob's Journey

"Off-road" vehicle

Journal Entry #17

Losing Traction

Bob and I thought we'd never get done with the Road Fork section in southeastern Ohio. As in the Shawnee section, it took four trips before I could finally stick a fork in it.

It began smoothly enough, at least as far as racking up the miles. On our first trip we logged 39 miles in three days; they were all on-road miles. Those may be the least used roads I have hiked yet. It was difficult for me to picture the days when big rigs prowled those byways in the quest for energy.

We were enjoying the beautiful weather and scenery for the second day when an ATV roared up behind us. The sturdily-built rider sized us up and, with measured politeness, asked what we were doing. I imagined the limitless potential for a snappy dialogue this situation would have provided for you. In your absence, Bob unknowingly seized the golden opportunity. He innocently said, "We are hiking the Buckeye Trail."

I looked at the rider and noticed his muscular neck and arms. He said, "The Buckeye Trail doesn't go through here."

Bob and I, like Tweedledee and Tweedledum, pointed in unison to a nearby telephone pole that displayed a prominent blue blaze.

The rider replied, "I see it, but it shouldn't be there. The Buckeye Trail doesn't go through here."

The comeback popped when Bob said, "Yes, it does. This is called the Stupid Loop."

Though the official designation is Wilderness Loop, "Stupid Loop" is merely an affectionate name used by some hikers for this rugged 115-mile loop that was added on to the BT in 2005. It consists of the Road Fork and Whipple sections. I once heard that the uncomplimentary name came from a section hiker inconvenienced by it in her pursuit of the trail's end.

I filled our new friend in on this information since the look of surprise in his eyes revealed that he had never heard the term before that day and was taken aback at Bob's response. I *have* heard the term, and *I* was taken aback at Bob's response. I looked at Mr. Buckeye-Trail-Doesn't-Go-Through-Here more closely. He was gaining muscle tissue even as I watched. He asked if we were carrying. We told him no. He said that we should probably start. Funny, I was thinking the same thing.

After his somber warnings of possible snakes, bears, coyotes, *boars?*, wolves, and other unspecified dangers along the road, we parted. An uneasy feeling accompanied us. If the man on the ATV meant to spook us, it had worked. He had not really been hostile, but it was obvious that he was not a Buckeye Trail Association promoter.

Bob and I walked on down the road with few words passing between us. After a while, movement in a field to our left drew my attention. My eyes locked on three large canines. We watched as they followed a fence line that ran parallel to the road. It must have been a hundred yards away, and from that distance, the creatures looked amazingly like coyotes. It appeared that they were measuring their steps to match ours.

We continued on, glancing occasionally at the dogs (or coyotes or wolves). They couldn't really be anything but huge dogs, but the earlier warning was still ringing in my ears. I've heard that fear can distort vision. No doubt, they could see us just fine; my vision, on the other hand, was beginning to blur. I did see, however, that the fence line began to gradually angle toward the road. I also saw the canines start to trot and narrow the distance between us.

Finally all three broke into a run and came straight at us. I call this our "coyote moment." We were still unsure of their objectives or of their species. If they had malicious intentions, we could put up little resistance. I had pepper spray, but there was no time to dig it out.

Maybe I got a little taste of the "wolves at my door" that you mentioned more than once the last few times I saw you. You never told me what the wolves were, but you must have felt that everything was closing in on you and you had no safe place to run. You often used vivid imagery, but this statement of yours had never impacted me so strongly as it did along that road in Road Fork.

Just as they got to the road, we could see that they were indeed dogs, two of them large pups. Mom stopped warily in the ditch; the other two ran up to us, but quickly rejoined their mother when we made a friendly gesture toward them. The mother was merely being protective. My pulse rate began its descent back to double digits.

After a much less eventful third day, we returned home. We had only 18 miles to finish in Road Fork, one more trip back for a two-day hike. We thought we might even get some miles done in the Whipple section.

It wasn't to be, though. Two weeks later we went back, only to be sent packing for home after seven miles due to flash floods in the area. We tried again after another couple of weeks. That time Bob became sick, and we got in even less mileage.

□ □ □

We finally made it back two months later with only 6.9 miles left, but without a great deal of confidence that we could finish even that in one trip.

We reached Wayne National Forest early in the evening, arriving in separate cars as usual. As darkness was falling, we drove down a gravel road looking for our camp. Ten minutes earlier, we had passed a line of monster trucks parked in front of one of the few houses out that way. (For a second I thought we had wandered into West Virginia.) It had looked as if a huge party was going on in the backyard. I was wishing I had one of those trucks as I slowly followed Bob up a large hill.

The road became muddy and deeply rutted. After a mile of sliding and spinning, Bob slid off the road—dangerously near a cliff. Each attempt to get back on the road moved him closer to the edge.

I doubted that AAA service even extended back that far, and even if it did, they probably couldn't have gotten a service vehicle in. Besides, our phones hadn't worked for miles. So Bob climbed in my car and we managed to backtrack, with Bob getting out to push whenever we got stuck. There was only one place to go.

It must have been about ten o'clock when we pulled into the party. My Caravan looked miniscule alongside those trucks, but it made a noble attempt at fitting in with its fresh coat of mud.

We approached the group and quickly explained that Bob's car was being swallowed up. Before we could elaborate, a fellow named Dave loaded us into his truck. He gave my Caravan a look of respect (or was it pity?) and we took off. Several trucks and ATVs followed.

Nobody could believe how far we had made it up the road. Dave explained that just the weekend before, an unofficial 4-wheeler marathon had taken place on that hill so that the local boys could "blow off some steam." The roads had not been repaired yet. Dave hooked his truck to the Journey, then gingerly tugged. Just as the car was about to "journey" over the hill, he gunned his engine and saved Bob's car from disaster.

During the entire rescue, no payment had been mentioned. They were just guys wanting to help, like people we have met all over the state. Bob did pay Dave, but it was obvious he would have done it for nothing.

We drove back down to get my car, declined a beer from the boys, and wished them the best as we set off for camp by another route. We were relieved to finally finish Road Fork the next day, but even more relieved to be back on solid ground.

RECENTLY I RAN ACROSS a folder of Dave's stories. He was always writing, and some of the pieces were over my head. Others were simpler and tugged at my heart, like this one about a happy time in his childhood.

> . . . I think I liked childhood better, though. I guess I was about seven before I discovered the truth about Santa. My ornery older brother just couldn't keep it in any longer; otherwise, I'd have probably been safe in the belief into my teens. Innocence was fun while it lasted. And Dad was quite upset at my brother for squealing. Pa was having fun putting on the red suit and sneaking around in the dark on Christmas Eve, strategically ensuring I'd catch just a glimpse from my bed now and then. Once that

jig was up he found his creative outlet in making me find my gifts, leaving small clues as Christmas approached. Soon mom was cheerfully joining in his devious conspiracies. One year I found the top half of my coveted graphite spinning rod serving as the trunk for that odd-looking, wispy little homemade Christmas tree mom set up in my room for some reason. She didn't give me the star for the top until Christmas morning; it was only when I peeled the makeshift brown paper off the top of the tree that I noticed the high-tech end grommet of the fishing rod. That star would have to wait another year. One time dad just wordlessly handed me the bulletin for the Christmas Eve candlelight service with that sneaky look in his eye which alerted me that the game was afoot. Now, surely he wouldn't use his position as pastor to manipulate the schedule of proceedings just to have some fun with his son! My candle was down to the nub before I realized that the first letter of every paragraph came together to spell 'IN THE FISH.' I raced home and carefully reached into the mouth of his prized mounted muskie, razor-sharp teeth and all (we weren't as safety conscious back then), only to find a note saying 'The other fish.' But there was only one fish! He wouldn't even look at me when he got home - it wasn't until the wee hours that I jumped out of bed to find my new skateboard on the front seat of his Plymouth Barracuda.

I can't remember who spilled the beans about Santa. Since I moved out four years before Lloyd, it is more likely that he was the culprit. I *do* remember that Christmas was a joyful time for all the kids—and adults—in the Spencer family.

In 2004 childhood was a distant memory. Dave became increasingly bogged down with routine responsibilities, just what it took to build up his business in Wayne County. He personally serviced the computers of a good percentage of his friends, some businesses, and even some city and county government buildings. From stringing lines in hot attics to troubleshooting elusive problems on PCs, it was tough work and long hours.

He was waiting for the year that his business would show a profit, but just when it looked as though it was going to happen, circumstances took a turn for the worse. Business fell off due to a slowdown in demand for computer services. At about the same time, the interest rate on his credit cards that he had maxed out on recent recreational excesses was skyrocketing.

Nevertheless, Dave always found a way to finance his vacations. He lived to get away once a year, usually for a couple of weeks, to totally escape the gripping tentacles of the computer business.

I felt that he was also trying to dig out of the depression I was seeing, but I wasn't sure if his vacation behavior helped or compounded this problem. On that Jamaican trip in 2007 where he mingled with the locals, the plan included a generous sampling of native beverages to the point of sometimes waking up not knowing where he was. One night he picked up a souvenir from the island: a shiny black eye. He was extremely proud of that and showed me a photo of it many times. Once would have been enough.

Each year he seemed to get a little more depressed in between vacations. That meant more alcohol and, eventually, more sleeping pills. Contributing to his downward spiral was the recent death of our mother. Dave seemed to be stuck somewhere in the middle of the grieving process.

I was always just a little jealous about how close Dave and Mom had been. It's not that Mom didn't love all of us, but when she said Dave's name, I often thought I saw a special twinkle in her eyes. Dave was the baby of the family, raised after Paula, Lloyd, and I had moved out, and in her estimation there was nothing he could do wrong.

Another trigger to Dave's increasing depression was the ending of his marriage. As part of the divorce agreement, he was obligated to make some home repairs so that the house could be sold and the proceeds divided. He talked to me about his plans and even began to gather supplies. However, he made few of the repairs. Instead he spent more and more time sitting on his back deck, gazing at the stream flowing by.

I understand depression. Studies show that it can run in some families; ours is one of them. It plagues me, but my strategy tends to be proactive. On a good day, I manage it rather than allow it to manage me. Dave was cut from a different cloth. He soaked himself in depression and became even more creative and introspective; he almost seemed to thrive on feeling blue.

What was that look in Dave's eyes as he sat in his Lazy Boy in his back yard? Where was the fun-loving soul he used to be? When would it be Christmas Day again? Dave was sliding off the road. . . but he always found a way to get back on.

CAESAR CREEK SECTION

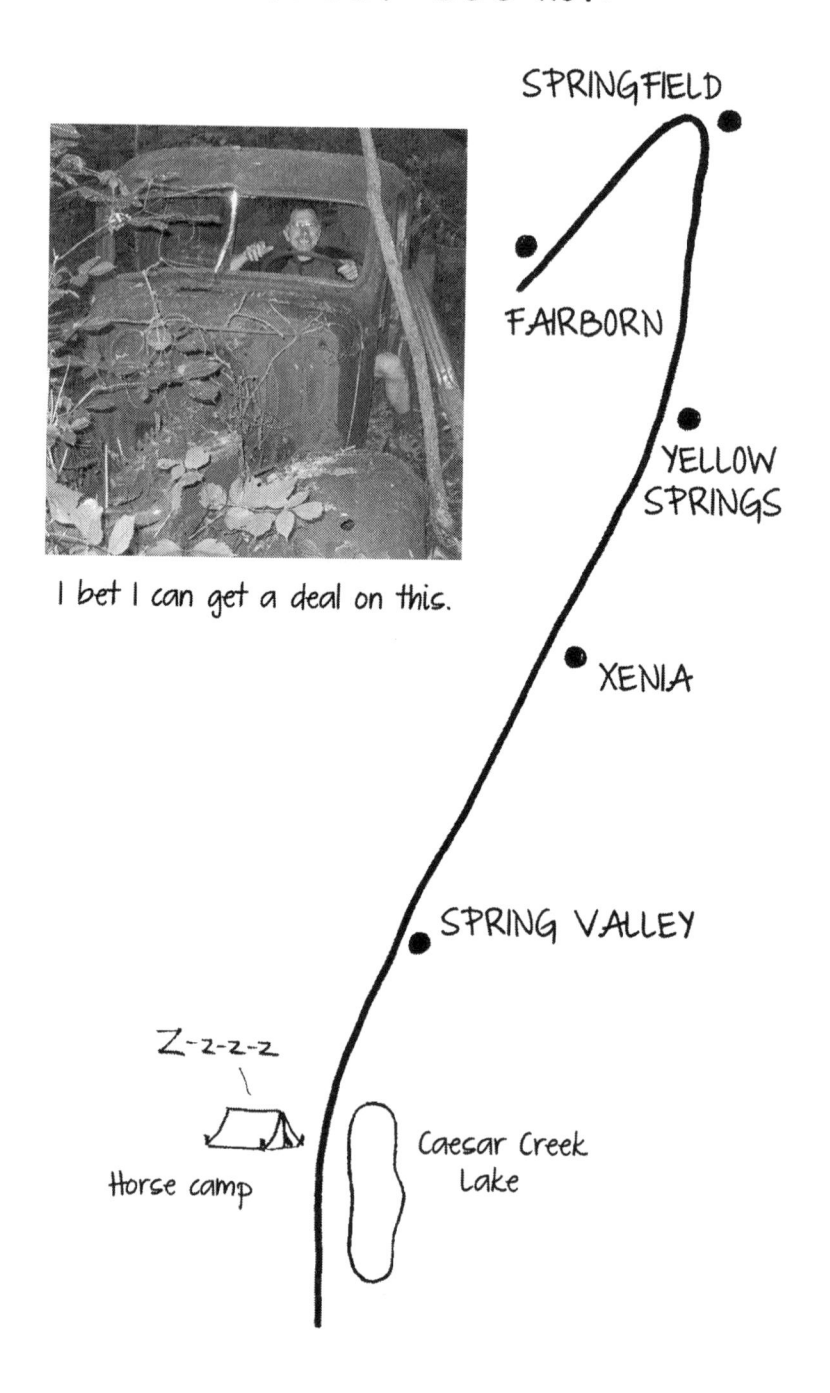

I bet I can get a deal on this.

SPRINGFIELD

FAIRBORN

YELLOW SPRINGS

XENIA

SPRING VALLEY

Z-z-z-z

Horse camp

Caesar Creek Lake

Journal Entry #18

Losing the Battle

The only vehicle I photographed on my hike in the Caesar Creek section had definitely seen better days. I always keep one eye out for old trucks—you know how they call out to me—but how I noticed this one, I'm not sure. It was a steamy day, and I was occupied primarily with just keeping the sweat and spider webs from my head and neck. The truck sat about a hundred feet off the trail and blended in beautifully with the surrounding foliage.

Jim and I carefully approached the abandoned treasure, pushing our way through long-undisturbed webs and weeds that engulfed it. I peered into the cab to make sure it was not occupied by any *other* truck-loving carnivores. Spotting no teeth, I climbed warily into what was left of the seat.

As I looked over the dash and the doors, my smile faded. The old workhorse was beyond any hope of restoration. I realized that no amount of Bondo, lead, cab corners, or loving care could bring it back. The vehicle was in far worse shape than any of the clunkers you or I have been blessed to disown. I was sure that the elements had reached the magic number.

As the afternoon sun continued to beat down on us that first day in Caesar Creek State Park, Jim and I traveled on, occasionally joking about "our truck." After rounding a few more turns, we were surprised to meet the first other people we had seen since we entered the park that morning. Their horses were even more surprised. One was so startled that it threw its rider off. Amazingly, she landed on her feet. After she assured us that neither her frame nor her feelings were damaged, we stood like statues while the riders cautiously passed by.

Fifty of the miles in this section were easy, mostly flat bike trails and roads winding past Spring Valley, Xenia, Yellow Springs, Springfield, and finally Fairborn. However, the twenty off-road miles in Caesar Creek State Park made for a strenuous, but invigorating, hike. I was looking forward that first day to getting to the horse camp where we would pitch our tents (if the horses weren't occupying all the sites).

We reached camp just before dark. As was usually the case when I slept out, I tossed and turned most of the night. A slight breeze cleared the air of some of the oppressive humidity. It was a good time to listen to the sounds of the woods: deer snorting, leaves rustling, tree frogs singing... and Jim snoring in the next tent. At least *someone* was getting some sleep. As I lay awake, I thought back to some of my BT experiences with him.

▫ ▫ ▫

When I met Jim on my first BT hike, I could tell that he was a man with patience, a listening ear, and a lot of quiet wisdom. I walked with him a lot that first hike, hoping that some of those traits would rub off on me. In my mind, I had been coming up quite short. I told him at that time why I was hiking the BT. He thought he pretty much understood how I was feeling.

Jim loved to talk about the Buckeye Trail Crew work parties—almost as much as he loved to attend them. At first, this made me wonder a bit about him. "Work party" made about as much sense to me as "sleeping out" or "slightly lost." He explained that volunteers would gather at preselected locations on the BT and do jobs such as dig out honeysuckle and multiflora rose, repair old trails, and build new ones. It just sounded like work to me. Besides, you know I'm not exactly Mr. Party. But I decided to go with him to an upcoming work party in the Scioto section anyway.

The group of volunteers who met in Scioto that day showed me how to put the "party" in work party. It started when another guy named Jim handed out all the tools. The safety rules were strict, but the way he delivered them was comedic. Humor can go a long way in getting a point across, and I think we all appreciated it.

When we got to the site, we were told that we could take all the breaks we wanted. The response to my surprised reaction was, "What's the worst that can happen if you take too many breaks? We cut your pay?" It kept getting better. Another partier was glad to be getting into the "free fitness club." In spite of the break policy and the constant joking, or maybe because of them, a lot of hard work took place and much was accomplished on the trail that day.

The hilarity continued that night after we ate at the chuck wagon and gathered around the fire. The sit-down comics kept us roaring harder than the blazing campfire. It made me miss your silly, off-the-wall humor. You would have been a hit with them, Dave. I mentioned that to Jim. Once again, it helped to have his listening ear.

▫ ▫ ▫

The sounds from Jim's tent died down, and my restless reflections were finally overtaken by sleep. In the morning John and Chris joined us. They are two active BTA trustees and men for whom I have a great deal of appreciation. All three men with me that day knew why I was hiking the BT and united their hearts with mine.

As we walked, I gave thought to why you left me. Will I ever know? I have seen someone thrown unexpectedly, yet still land on her feet and continue on. I have seen that washed-out trails can be restored with the right tools and can realize the purpose for which they were created. But maybe you felt like that old truck, just sitting there rusting into the soil, too far gone to fix and restore.

D AVE CALLED ME EARLY in the spring of 2008. He was taking some time off for a trip to Watoga State Park and wanted me to join him. When I said I would come, he sarcastically responded that I probably didn't think it was important enough to get there on time. I had been a couple of days late the other time we vacationed there. Usually Dave's light sarcasm was funny to me; this time it had some bite to it and irked me. It irked me enough to get me to the park early, which was probably his plan in the first place.

Dave was becoming moodier and darker. I wondered when he was going to pull out of the blackness. I had no doubt that he would; it just seemed to be taking him longer than usual this time.

From the beginning of the week, he complained of headaches and lack of appetite. Appetite had never seemed a problem for him before. He also thought he had a brain tumor. I suggested that he get a checkup, but he changed the subject. After that we argued about something insignificant, then gave each other the cold shoulder for the rest of the day. Our week was not starting off well.

That changed suddenly when I woke up on day three to the smell of fresh coffee and the sound of an AM talk show that I liked and Dave hated. That was a big surprise. When I entered the kitchen, Dave was pouring the steaming brew into my mug. He said he was feeling better. Later he suggested that we go to the Dairy Queen for lunch, so we took off.

Dave got the biggest burger with the most toppings, along with a milkshake and large fries. He got sick on the way back to the cabin and explained that he had not eaten much in the previous week, that food hadn't tasted very good to him lately. However, he made it clear that he was glad he had feasted on a giant burger one last time. The statement seemed odd, but at the time, I figured that he meant he had learned his lesson and would watch his diet more carefully in the future.

Since Dave and I were not exactly big gun owners, any discussion of firearms usually revolved around the political aspect. Dave had talked for the last year or two, though, about getting one for protection. I didn't think twice about it until he showed me his handgun that he'd brought with him. I think he said it was a .357 Magnum. He had taken classes and gotten his permit. He *was* serious about this protection thing. I knew that we both had an excessive fear of bears, but a gun?

I did a lot of hiking by myself that week while Dave sat on the front porch of the cabin and drank. I knew that he needed these escape times, and as much as I was concerned about him, I'd seen him use this process many times to get back on top of things.

When Dave would finally come in at night, he slept on the couch in the living room while I enjoyed the bedroom. I insisted that we should each get the bedroom for half the week. He replied that he would let me know if and when he needed it. He never did.

Before our week was up, out of the blue he said he had to get back and catch up on his work. I was disappointed to leave early, but was relieved to see the renewed initiative he was showing.

I told Dave I would follow him back as far as his turnoff near Huntington. He had decided to take a different, more scenic, route, one I had never traveled. Since I was just following, I can't recall exactly what the route was, but we passed through what I thought was some of the most beautiful country in the state. I was enjoying the snow crested hills and almost drove past Dave's van that was pulled over by the guardrail.

I managed to slow quickly enough to pull in behind him. As he walked back and peered into my open window, I could tell that he was extremely shaken. He said he had almost been run off the road and asked if I had seen the near catastrophe. No, I hadn't. He told me that he thought he was a goner. The close call had awakened him to how important life was and he didn't want to die; he wanted to live. Then he asked me not to tell his girlfriend about the close call.

Back on the highway, I ran Dave's words through my mind over and over trying to make them add up, but each time I did I came up with a different answer. The entire week, I had been locked in a strange zone where nothing made sense. I had never heard Dave say that he wanted to die, so why was he now saying that he didn't? Why the drastic mood swings? If he thought he had a brain tumor, why not get it checked out?

Something was seriously wrong, but I couldn't figure out how to help my kid brother. I couldn't even wrap my brain around the problem—always the first step to getting to a solution.

I wanted to tell Dave that God could reverse this process, that He could help him to eventually land on his feet, that He could take the ruin of his life and repair it. I knew from personal experience that it was true. God had found me rusting alongside the trail, looking like a lost cause, but not too far gone for Him to restore.

I didn't want to preach. Dave had scolded me a time or two in the past about that. I just wanted to give him hope. But I feared it would sound to Dave like another lecture and be rejected, so I continued to silence my concerns, bottle up my feelings, and hope for the best.

OLD MAN'S CAVE SECTION

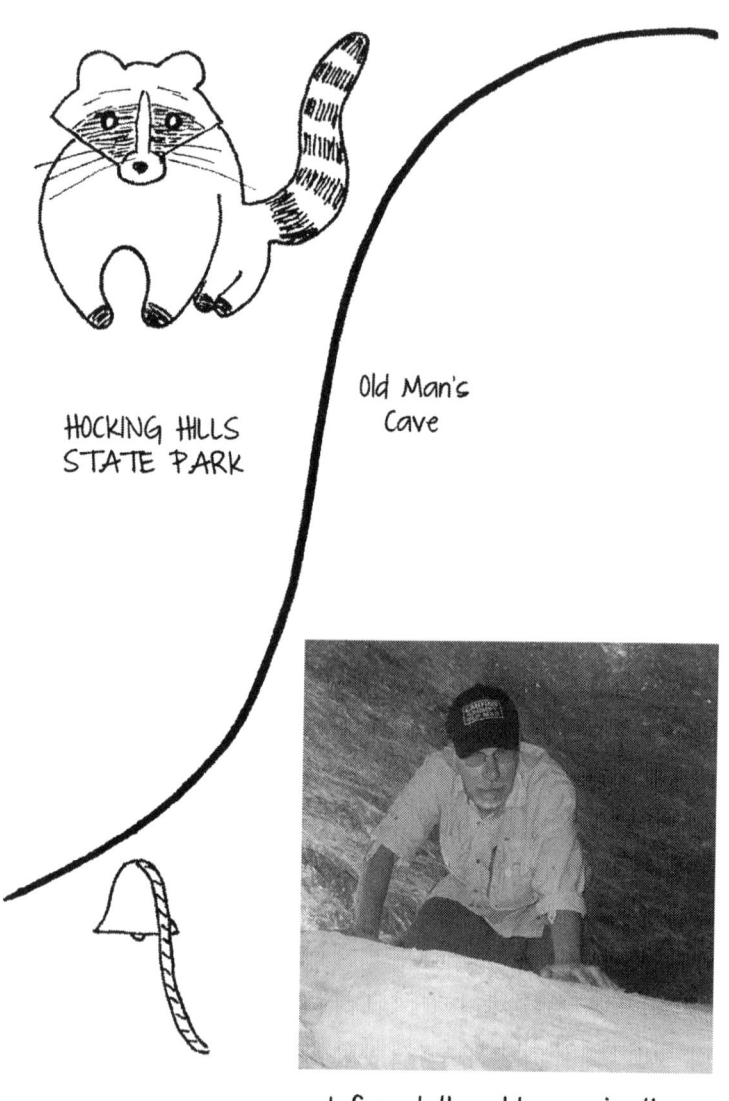

HOCKING HILLS STATE PARK

Old Man's Cave

I found the old man in the cave . . . and he was me.

Journal Entry # 19

Finding My Role

PREHIKE ENTRY—I was listening more closely than usual to the AM radio commercial. You know, the one that promises a fountain of youth in a bottle. It sounded good at first, but fortunately I came to my senses before I ordered the magic elixir. I realized that, even if the promise was real, I don't want to relive my youth. One time was definitely enough. Better off with who I am now. Besides, I didn't think it would make much of a difference in one week.

Why did the commercial capture my attention this time when I've heard it so many times before? I've been preparing for a backpacking trip through almost 40 miles of the Old Man's Cave section, and part of my prep is my usual round of worrying. I heard that Darryl's hikes are fast and fun. I also caught wind of a rumor that the group that would assemble for this hike would consist mostly of 20-somethings and that there would be a lot of them. I'm sure they all will probably have those shoes that look like feet and underwear that wicks and breathes. I will be putting the "old man" into the Old Man's Cave hike. I gotta go. I have to run to the drug store and try to find some powdered prune juice and maybe some of that "Just for Old Men."

▫ ▫ ▫

THE HIKE—I showed up wearing a "CAUTION-GRUMPY OLD MAN" cap. What the logo really meant was, "Please like me and include me in the group." I know, that's a strange way to say it. But it's a big deal for me to hike with people I don't know, especially for three days. How would I fit in? I couldn't remember ever being the oldest on a hike. Being a confirmed Golden Retriever, I spend way too much time worrying if people will like me.

I surveyed the group as we gathered at our starting point. Worry had worked again: 90 percent of what I worry about doesn't happen. There was no age gap, just a nice range from around 30 to 60-ish. I had pictured a massive group of twenty or thirty, but we had the perfect number of seven. I say perfect because I have a hard time connecting with many more than that at one time.

One of the group members was Bob (not Zombie Bob) whom I had hiked with once before. It was great to see a familiar face, and someone even older than me. Dori had also been worried that she would be the oldest. It worked for her too: Bob and I would share the role of being the senior hikers.

Michelle was younger than Dori. She had never backpacked before, and her pack weighed more than ours did on the AT! I couldn't wait to see if she might be lugging a hibachi. Craig and his friend Brian were young as well. They didn't have toe shoes, and I didn't ask about their underwear. In fact, I later learned that Craig shops the box stores for some of his hiking apparel. Darryl acted as if he had always known me, even though we had talked only a couple of minutes a few weeks before. My pre-hike apprehensions were dwindling.

The advisory that Darryl hikes fast was true. He took two steps to my three, and covered more ground. However, he usually stationed either Craig or Brian behind as "sweepers." They stayed back with the slowpokes and walked from person to person making sure everybody was

OK. Sometimes Darryl took a turn at sweeping. Nobody pressured us. We all were able to hike our own hike.

From the first funny wisecrack, Brian made me think of you. I knew that we had at least one Otter on the trip. He also likes hard exercise as much as you did. When he wasn't sweeping, he was hiking extra miles, sometimes racing up and down the same hills or stairways two or three times. Many times Craig would join him. All the while, those two would be bantering and joking back and forth.

When Michelle dumped her bag of food out on the picnic table at camp that first night, I found out why her pack was so heavy. No hibachi, but just like us on the AT, she was making sure she wouldn't run out of vittles. She probably could have fed our entire group.

Brian and Craig hung their food in the trees, but I had forgotten my rope and was too proud to ask for help. Besides, I had never had my tent raided before, so I took my food into the vestibule with me when I retired.

The resident raccoons must have sympathized with Michelle's plight. They came during the night and relieved her of much of her load. When she discovered them, she shooed them over to my tent for their next course. I saw one peeking in and grumped at it. I must have terrified it, because it scampered a whole five feet away. When I crawled out and yelled at it some more, it sauntered another five feet. I chased that marauding masked mammal away from my tent several more times during the next couple of hours.

The Spanish word for raccoon is *mapache*, originally from the Nahuatl *mapachitli* of the Aztecs, and means "the one who takes everything in its hands." I was determined that it wouldn't take *my* everything. I briefly considered putting my food in the sleeping bag with me, but I didn't want to take a chance on waking up with a furry bagmate.

Instead, I relocated my food bag to the shower house around two o'clock in the morning, hoping the would-be raider couldn't get the door open. I guess my role that night was being the raccoon magnet.

The next day Brian, Craig, and I hung back from the rest of the group so that I could shoot some pictures. When we entered Old Man's Cave, I felt right at home.

The original old man in the cave, who was reportedly buried there in the nineteenth century, was actually the younger brother, Richard Howe. While on a trip to the Ozarks, he discovered that his older brother David had passed away. Wanting to help out his Native American sister-in-law, he returned home to dig up some money he had stashed in the gorge. As he was breaking the ice in a river near the gorge with the butt of his musket, the weapon discharged and killed him. Later, trappers found him and buried him somewhere in the cave. Looks like brotherly loyalty like ours goes back quite a ways in these parts. Mothers would tell their children about the ghost of the old man, hoping this would keep them away from the edges of the steep cliffs and drop-offs. Or so one of the stories goes.

When it came time to leave the cave, we double-timed it to catch the rest of the group at Cedar Falls. Our final destination stood 18 miles from where we had started that morning. Michelle and Dori were getting into the groove, good-naturedly complaining to Darryl about the distance. I enjoyed the group chemistry.

Brian went back and forth again, encouraging and motivating the "Floundering Four." Bob's hip hurt, and my foot was killing me. Michelle was nearing her endurance limit, and Dori was having problems with the road-walking piece. Even Darryl looked like he might be tiring. Brian and Craig appeared to be more energized than ever.

That night Michelle made the decision to end her hike. Before she got a ride back to her car the next morning, e-mail addresses and hugs were exchanged as our group said goodbye to her and our awesome trail angels, Byron, Shannon, and Jamie. Michelle had done fine, I thought, considering her inexperience, her ill-fitting shoes, and her ultra-heavy backpack. That was you and me on our first backpacking trip, so I tried to show her a lot of empathy. My favorite role to a tee.

The ten or so miles to where Jim would pick me up were hot and hilly, but we found trail magic again halfway through. We asked a man sitting on his porch if he knew of a shady place we could eat. He directed us to the tiny church across the road. It felt about 60 degrees inside, looked tidy, and reminded me a whole lot of one of Dad's first churches. I was actually eating in the sanctuary, but this time I think Dad would have understood. The words "Mind God" were on the pulpit—just as they had been on Dad's favorite cap—sending me on a nostalgia trip.

I noticed the mischievous look in Brian's eyes as he contemplated the rope on the old church bell. *Otter alert!* He gripped the pew ahead of him and, fortunately, choked back the temptation to ring the bell. It must have been the admonition on the pulpit.

The hike turned out great. Besides the breathtaking scenery of this section, I appreciated the easy camaraderie and the fun conversations. I especially enjoyed listening to Brian, Darryl, and Craig as they joked and razzed each other.

I didn't say a lot since I'm not always quick with a response. For the most part, I just enjoyed the humor. The chemistry reminded me of you, Lloyd, Dad, and me. Once again I was back in the role of the quiet but appreciative audience.

LLOYD, PAULA, AND I were all older than Dave, but I was the oldest. I took seriously my role of looking out for him. Sometimes I still called him Li'l Dave, even when he became taller and more muscular than me. Dave, and Paula too, would call me Big Brother, a name I relished.

We didn't often all get together. In fact, the four of us hadn't reunited since our mother's funeral in 2003. However, Dave, Lloyd, and I were at the nursing home in 2005 for Dad's 80th birthday.

At the party, Lloyd and Dad joked and bantered as usual. Dave joined in with his quick and witty one-liners. Their wisecracks always came across as funny; I could say the same thing and it would sound mean. A couple of times I did get in a good line, but for the most part I was content with my role of being a supportive audience.

I have given much thought to the makeup of my family. To me, our middle brother Lloyd appeared to be the most successful in building a good life, but it seemed as though Dave looked more to me for guidance. Though honored, I didn't feel like the best person to give it. After traveling a rocky road to my teaching degree and weathering a 13-year marriage that eventually ended, I didn't consider myself to be a qualified mentor.

I was unsure of how to react to Dave's behavior as of late, especially after our curtailed vacation in Watoga. We hadn't met to hike at Shawnee since then. When we communicated, his mood seemed to rise and fall like the coasters at the local amusement park. One moment he would be joking, the next, in a funk.

Sometimes I felt as if he was playing a game with me. I was torn. Should I let Dave hike his own hike and just be there for support, or should I initiate some serious big brother intervention?

The latter would be a difficult undertaking for me. I didn't feel like the ideal role model, and I worried about what Dave thought of me. I had started to run post-game analysis on the success or failure of almost every conversation we had. I wanted to make sure that Dave saw me as open-minded and didn't view me as the old fogy.

Dave was sharing his feelings more, and he seemed to be searching for answers. He was opening his life up to me in a way he never had before. It was time for me to reciprocate, and I didn't want to blow it. But it seemed more than ever as if we were communicating on different wavelengths. Most of the time, I didn't even understand his questions.

WHIPPLE SECTION

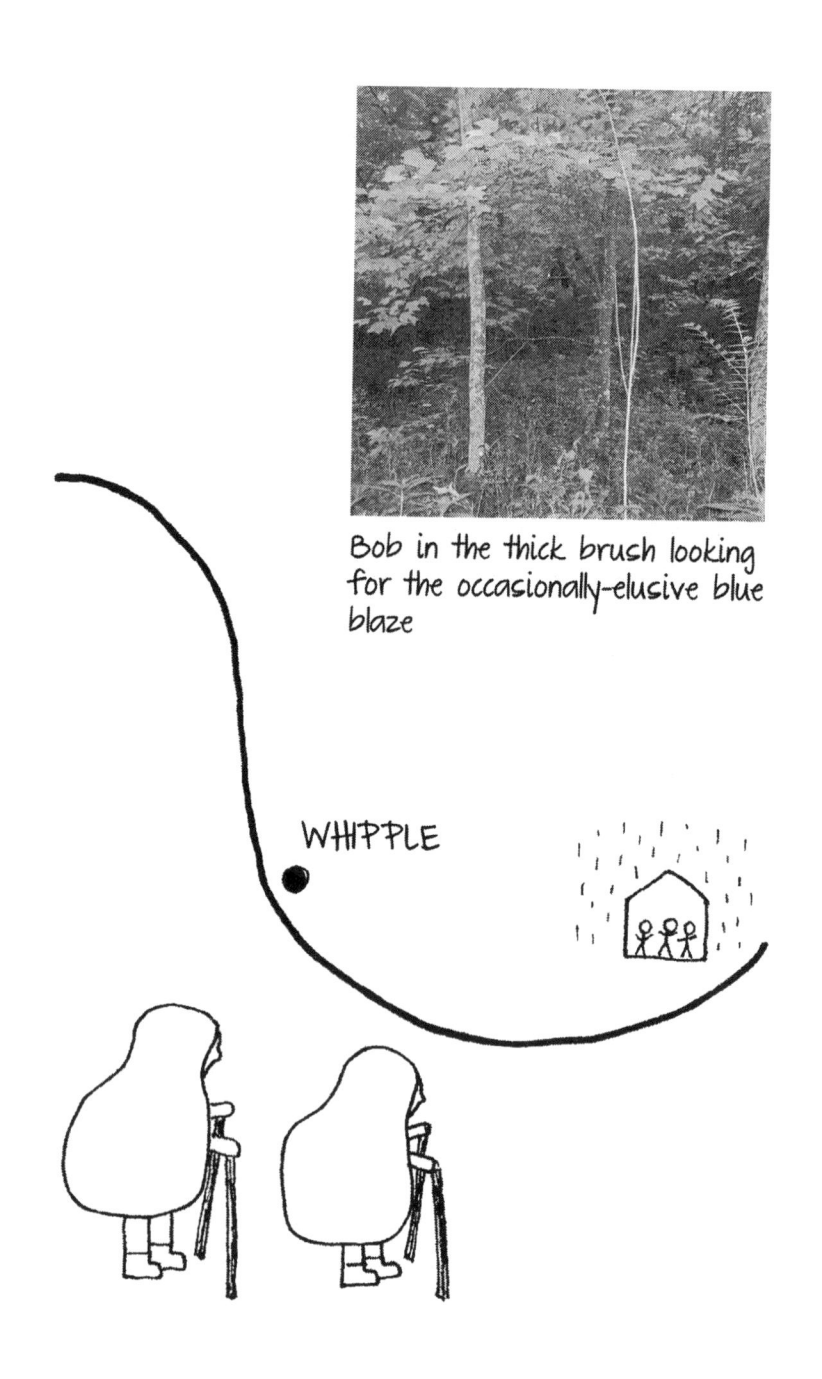

Bob in the thick brush looking for the occasionally-elusive blue blaze

WHIPPLE

Journal Entry #20

Losing the Way

Where was Bob? My eyes scoured the brush, but there was no sign of him. That part of the Whipple section had swallowed up my friend. I finally spotted him flailing in the overgrowth. He was trying to find a blaze, a tread—any sign of the Buckeye Trail.

Over the previous three miles, we had found only a few traces of it, barely enough to continue. We reached a place, however, where we were basically clueless. Being a trail maintainer, I understand how quickly a trail can become impassible, if not invisible. I had given up. Bob, on the other hand, wasn't quite ready to surrender to the besieging vegetation. I stood and watched Bob scuffle with the bushes for a while.

When he had been sufficiently scratched, poked, bruised, and bloodied, he bullied his way back out of the brush and consented to join me in bushwhacking down toward the road. A storm was whipping up, a nasty one according to the radio, so we covered our packs and hoped for the best. The trees were already creaking loudly against the force the winds were imposing on them, and the smell of rain promised us a heavy soaking shortly.

We spotted a shed, raising our hopes that we would have shelter before the skies opened up. Several large dogs bounded out of the structure and raced toward us. I was thankful to see that just behind them was the owner of the property. He guided us into the sanctuary just in time. Introductions were made. His last name sounded familiar. We quickly found out why when he asked if we were "the boys" whom his son had rescued from the muck a couple of weeks earlier. That family seemed to be in the business of keeping Bob and me high and dry.

While chatting with Jerold and his wife, we learned that we hadn't been far off when we were looking for the trail. It was located about a hundred yards up the hill. We had actually crossed over it coming down the old oil truck road that led by their house.

We waited out the storm, which lasted long enough to raise the creek at the edge of the property over its banks, and then we decided we would have to settle for the measly three miles we had hiked that morning. It would have been hard enough to hack our way through the trail under normal conditions; in such disagreeable weather, and when we couldn't even find the trail, it would have been nearly impossible.

We said our goodbyes and started down the road. When we had gone only a short way, Jerold pulled up behind us. He loaded us and our gear into his compact car (which could have fit into, or maybe even under, the bed of his son's truck) and drove us to Bob's car. Once again, we headed home with miserably few miles logged.

A few days later, Bob called me with some advice given to him by a BT trustee on how to get through the overgrown part of Whipple. He had given Bob the official OK to follow the road past those six or seven miles of trail. I thought that was sound advice. Bob, however, thought differently. He was determined to do it right. He was going to go back and find the trail, or else blaze a new one himself. Since he was my friend, I agreed to help him in his endeavor—but only grudgingly after a serious debate with myself.

I saw you in your own personal jungle, Dave, tangled in the overgrowth, looking for a sign that would lead you back to the desired path of your life. When you couldn't find it, you settled on a detour of alcohol and medication. Maybe what you needed was someone to go with you into your jungle, someone with the appropriate knowledge and tools, to help you blaze your way out. I'm sorry, Dave, that I didn't stay and help you make that happen.

MY WIFE HAS BEEN READING through my manuscript. When she got to this chapter, she asked me why I had left out some of the details. It isn't easy to talk about the biggest and stupidest mistake of my life. But if it will help one person avoid the same mistake, it's worth revealing everything. Here is exactly what I remember about Memorial Day weekend, 2008.

It was Saturday and I was on my way to East Fork State Park. It was my turn to lead the camper church service the next morning. I was going to spend a few hours that afternoon inviting campers to the service—but then I got a call from Dave and my plans were left on the shoulder of eastbound Rt. 32.

Dave told me that I needed to come to West Virginia. I informed him that I was otherwise engaged, this was a big weekend at the park, and I would come Sunday afternoon. He responded that it couldn't wait; he felt like he was going to die and this was his "cry for help." It sounded as though he was heavily medicated. I turned the car around, grabbed some things at home, and headed back east to West Virginia.

For those three hours on the road, I kept telling myself, *No, not Dave*. I had always found a way through or around the "suffocating jungle" periods in my own life. I was sure Dave would as well. I didn't know anyone more capable of doing anything he wanted to do.

Although I was relieved to finally pull into Dave's drive, I dreaded what I would find. As I made my way to the back yard, my anxiety rose as high as the pile of empty beer cans lying beside the Lazy Boy. Dave looked listless and lost.

I tried to start a conversation, but he was too intoxicated to respond with much more than "Hi, thanks for coming." He surprised me by reaching over and grabbing my hand. We sat and watched the stream flow by for quite some time.

Desperately wanting to do something, I asked Dave if he was ready to go get some help. My heart dropped to my feet when he looked me in the eyes and slowly uttered, "Just look at me. There's no use." That look still haunts me to this day.

We spent most of Saturday night watching TV. Dave especially watched for news about the Phoenix lander that was approaching Mars.

Sunday morning came, and I was praying that I could help Dave make some kind of a breakthrough. Since we both had a long history of being in church on this day of the week, I steered the conversation to things of a spiritual nature. Dave assured me that "me and Uncle Jesus are cool."

He quickly changed the subject and said, "I can't believe I am going to say this to my big brother, but you know what? You are like a hamster in a wheel. You need to step out there, Squooge." *Step out where?* I didn't know where it was that I was supposed to be stepping out to. I couldn't get a direct answer from him. Then he dropped the subject as suddenly as he had brought it up and just sat staring across the water. It seemed as though Dave was playing games again, and I was not in the mood.

That entire weekend my brother and I seemed to be locked in some sort of alternative universe. My rules of logic did not apply there. One strange thing happened after another. While I was trying to process one odd behavior, another would crop up. It was as if I were being sucked into a black hole, a suffocating place from which I couldn't escape. I had never felt so helpless.

I could not respond in real time to what was happening. I thought I was hallucinating when I heard Dave ask me to hide his gun to get him through to the next day. I was so bewildered that I can't remember exactly what I did with it, but I made sure it was out of sight.

Shortly after that, Dave said we would go together the following day to get him admitted somewhere—anywhere—to get help. That was a positive change I needed to cling to, not only for Dave's well-being, but for my own sanity as well.

I was relieved when Monday, Memorial Day, finally arrived. Dave surprised me again when he appeared sober and in greatly improved spirits. He was particularly excited that the lander had safely touched down on the Red Planet around midnight. He said he wanted to stay home, get some food in him, and get some color back in his face. He told me he had just wanted to spend the weekend with me and now he was good. He was ready to get back to work.

I needed more than his abrupt mood swing to accept his backing out on getting the help he needed. I questioned him about all of his dark talk the last couple of days. He said he had been depressed because of the stomach cancer he thought he had, but he felt so good right then that maybe his stomach was all right. What about his speculations that he might die soon? He assured me that if he did die, it would be from natural causes only.

In spite of my initial skepticism concerning Dave's sudden rebound, he was able to convince me that he was better. I had seen him make a similar remarkable comeback in Watoga two months before. Although I was greatly disappointed that he wouldn't be getting into treatment that day, maybe I could talk him into it in the near future. After all, Dave was a 47-year-old man, old enough to make his own decisions. Right?

When the weekend had begun, my plan was to return home Monday, but I hadn't anticipated such bizarre and disturbing events. I was not comfortable about leaving Dave.

He maintained that he would never do anything to hurt himself because he knew what it would do to me. He was a salesman, and I was always buying. As proof that he was the ultimate pitchman—and I was the ultimate sucker—when Dave asked for his gun back, I gave it to him. To ease my apprehension, he gave me the sole bullet that the gun had housed and said not to worry.

In response to my continued hesitancy to leave, Dave insisted that he was OK and that I should go. I grudgingly conceded, but told him that I would be back in a couple of days. We hugged—our first real hug ever—and I walked to the car.

Another book was on my seat. Not by Louis L'Amour this time, but by Dave's favorite author, Steinbeck. It seemed as though I had already read *Travels with Charley*, as much as Dave had talked about it the last few visits. *Wow, what a gift!* I held up the book as I waved goodbye.

DEFIANCE SECTION

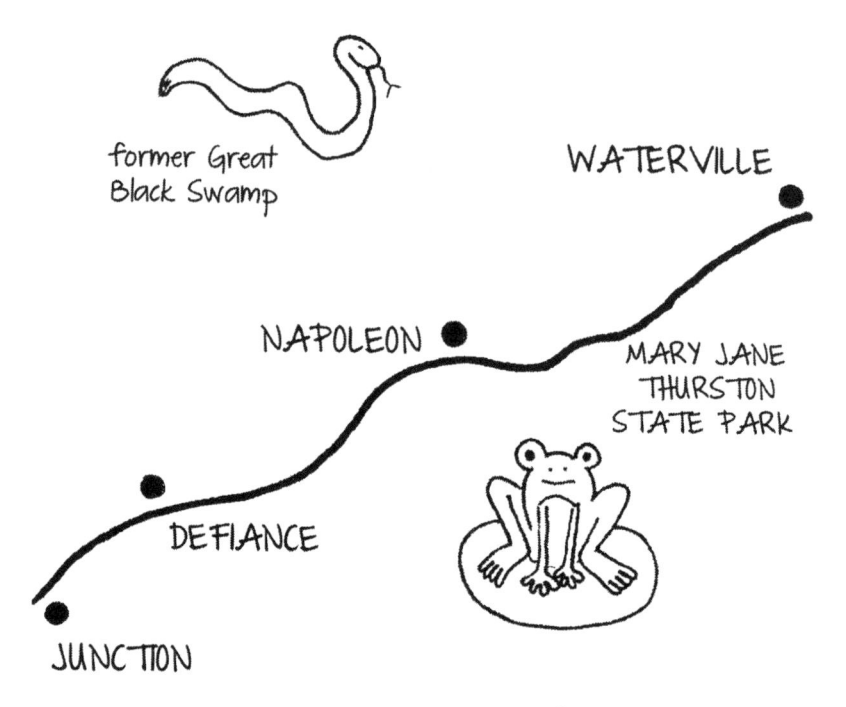

former Great Black Swamp

WATERVILLE

NAPOLEON

MARY JANE THURSTON STATE PARK

DEFIANCE

JUNCTION

A stone monument east of Defiance along SR 424

Journal Entry #21

Finding False Assurance

As I walked on the trail along the Maumee River east of Defiance in the Defiance section, historical plaques and my trusty *Follow the Blue Blazes* reminded me that countless others had left their footprints on the very same path over the last few centuries: Native Americans fighting to protect their land, U.S. soldiers fighting to protect the white settlers, black slaves fleeing to Canada, slave catchers following closely behind, and builders of the "twin canal" working feverishly to connect Indiana and western Ohio to Lake Erie. Quite a busy place, and that's just up until the mid-nineteenth century.

This would have been a dark and dreary place to hike in the 1700s and early 1800s. It was aptly named the Great Black Swamp. Things lurked in the standing water under the huge trees. You and I would have had fun exploring it, though we might have had some issues with the snakes and mosquitoes. My only aggravations that day were the high temperature and the humidity (and needing to find a Port-A-John every once in a while).

White settlers did not flock here at first, partly because of the swamp and partly because the American Indians had been promised that area of the state in the Treaty of Greenville. But we know that didn't last. I wonder how the Native Americans felt when, after being restricted first to west of the Appalachians, then to north of the Ohio River, and then to northwestern Ohio, the white settlements continually encroached into their territory. I'm torn. I'm glad the land now belongs to the U.S., but at the same time, I find myself rooting for the Indians (and I don't mean the baseball team our northern relatives are partial to).

The BT follows the Wabash and Erie Canal towpath, or what is left of it, through much of the section, which runs from Junction to Waterville. I didn't hike straight through from one end to the other. I jumped all over the place, hiking clockwise one day and counterclockwise the next. It took me two trips for a total of five days. On three of those days I traveled alone using the ole hike-bike method, one day I hiked 18 miles with Jim, and on the other I walked 10 miles to where Bob picked me up. I camped at Mary Jane Thurston State Park in McClure six times, four of those by myself. I wouldn't mind going back there to camp again, if just to listen to the frogs croaking along the Maumee at night.

As I hiked I tried to picture a canal boom town in tiny places like Junction and Independence. They must have been promising sites for investors. That is, until the canals gave way to faster modes of transportation.

When the swamps were drained and cleared in the late nineteenth century, farms popped up everywhere. Because of the needed rain, I'm sure the skies were being watched closely by the tillers of the former swampland. The rains predicted to occur while I was hiking didn't come. I heard that this was the country's worst drought since '56, and I was inclined to believe it. Golf balls were disappearing into the huge cracks at a local golf course, or so I overheard.

I met many nice people in this section. Mike, a local optometrist, gave me directions while he was out walking his dog. He then met me in Napoleon to make sure that I had followed them successfully. A mechanic named Willie stashed my bike in his garage. A stooped, white-haired gentleman at McDonald's in Defiance stopped by my table and chatted, as it seemed he did with everyone in the restaurant, wishing me luck when he heard about my hike. I want to be like him when I'm old and stooped: friendly and outgoing, imparting McBites of wisdom and encouragement.

But my thoughts kept drifting back to the people who had walked that path many years before, to travelers like Blue Jacket, a Shawnee war chief, who had journeyed along the Maumee on his way to the Grand Indian Council. There he and others worked to form alliances to try to stop westward expansion of the settlers. Because of the numerous broken promises already experienced, the council leaders just weren't trusting of the latest treaty—and who could blame them.

AS I STARTED TOWARD HOME on Memorial Day, I rolled the facts over and over in my mind. One of those facts was that Dave had also called Paula on Saturday, and they had made plans for her to come down to visit him Monday morning. Although Dave had told me that morning that Paula didn't need to come now, still I felt relieved that she would be arriving shortly and spending some time with him. Due to car trouble, however, she was forced to delay her trip. This was crucial information that Dave and I were both unaware of at the time.

I had also been encouraged by the fact that Dave had decided to wash a load of clothes on Sunday. I thought he was getting back into the right frame of mind to get some work done. It seemed like an especially good sign considering all the work one load of laundry demanded from him. Because of lingering plumbing problems in that end of the house, he had to carry buckets of water from the bathroom and across the house until the washer had finished all of its cycles.

Despite these promising signs, I was still uneasy. About five miles down the road, I pulled my car over to make some phone calls. First I talked with Bonnie. She was also concerned about Dave, but like me, she didn't think that he would do anything drastic. Then I called Jay, one of Dave's best friends. I questioned if I should leave Dave alone. We discussed the possibility of some type of intervention in the next few days.

We shared the changes we had both seen in Dave. He had been on a beer binge for several weeks, and added to that was a steady diet of sleeping pills. He had been using Ambien for quite some time. His depression had become much more severe since Mom died, which was understandable, but that was back in 2003. Even with all of this, we still didn't think that Dave would hurt himself. Jay said he would get over and visit in the next day or two.

I said goodbye, closed the phone, and continued the three-hour drive home. Still not at ease, I pulled over a couple of more times, trying to decide whether to turn around or to keep heading west. *Dave is looking and acting so much better today. Paula should arrive any minute. Jay knows about the situation and will be checking in on him. And I will be going back in a couple of days.* I continued west.

After I arrived home, I discussed with Bonnie all the things that Dave had said and done over the course of the weekend. I was hurting for and with Dave, but I thought—and hoped—that spending the weekend together had helped ease his depression. He certainly had been unusually open and expressive with me. I had been moving in that direction lately as well. When we hugged each other, I realized that we were both in a new place in our relationship. What I didn't know was that our first hug would also be our last.

I almost called Jay before I went to bed that night but decided to wait until morning. As I drifted uneasily to sleep, I was forming a plan to get something started in the way of an intervention. A picture was coming into focus, and my dreams that night did not take me to any pleasant places.

The Call came the next morning before I had the chance to make mine. Instant replays of that call still occur in my mind, even with the passage of over six years. Jay said that sometime Monday Dave had hurt himself.

I shuddered. "But . . . he's OK . . . right?"

"Clarence," Jay answered slowly and painfully, "Dave took his life . . . I'm sorry."

No! Not Dave!!

Part Three

Finding
Hope and Healing

AKRON SECTION

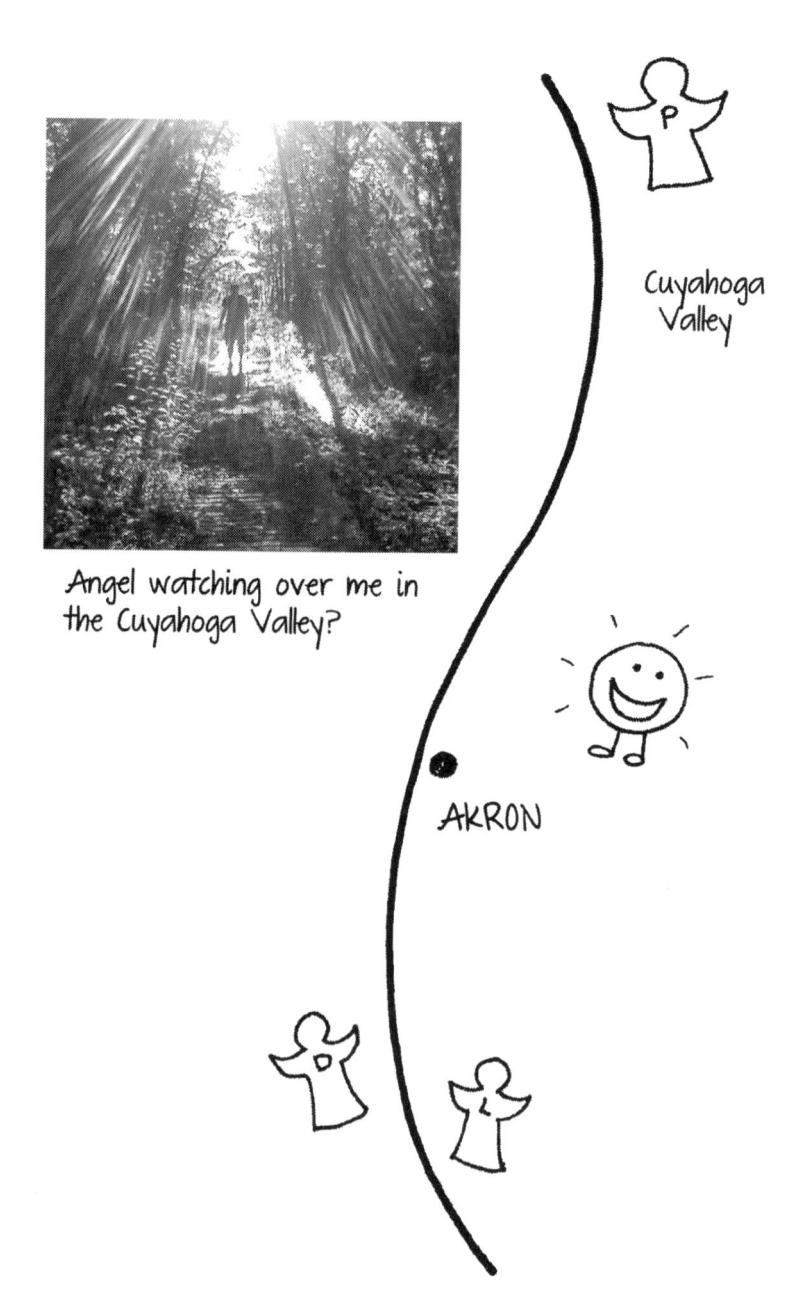

Angel watching over me in the Cuyahoga Valley?

Cuyahoga Valley

AKRON

Journal Entry #22

Finding Unexpected Blessings

Most of our Spencer clan would probably acknowledge the independent streak that clearly marks us. Normally, you and I wouldn't ask for help even if we were drowning in our own gene pool. Occasionally, though, I get that a big-time change is needed.

Since I began hiking the Buckeye Trail, I have been learning to take all the help I can get when it comes to planning, navigating, and keeping my head on straight enough to stay on the trail. In the Akron section, that help came in the form of many trail angels—maybe even a heavenly being or two.

I met two of those angels on a Saturday hike with a fairly large group of others who needed to complete miles in that section. Dana and Lisa had everything planned out for everyone who showed up. All we had to do was appear at the designated starting point on time. They also were our guides on the towpath trek and organized the shuttle back to our cars when we finished. I especially appreciated their periodic bathroom-location updates. (Maybe it's time to take the doc's advice on the Flomax).

Dana and Lisa regularly assist hikers passing through their section. More than once, they offered to be available whenever I returned. I told them why I was hiking and they extended words of encouragement. I couldn't have found better trail guides.

While up north later on a visit with Paula, I took it upon myself to get some miles in without the help of Dana and Lisa. I considered calling them at the last minute, but I told myself they might not be as spur-of-the-moment as you and I were. I determined to do this piece on my own, or so I thought.

I soon found myself in a pickle on the city streets of Akron. I was having trouble reading the map and became lost. To add to the problem, I really needed to find a bathroom, so I asked for directions from a man at the bus stop. He gestured toward the bar behind me with a disgusted look like, how could I not see it. I ran to the door but found it locked, so I carried on. *Smarty Pants.*

Even though I didn't see any blazes, I sure was making good time. I ended up in a blighted neighborhood, nervous, overhydrated, and kind of grumpy because of the snarky bus rider. At that moment, I was secretly hoping he had missed his bus.

Funny how we judge people by the neighborhoods they happen to live in or by what they wear. I was doing a lot of snap judging that day as an unfriendly-appearing man approached me on the sidewalk. He was obviously a resident of that area of town; I'm sure it was obvious to him that I wasn't.

I desperately needed to find a blaze, a bathroom, and a way to stop wandering from the trail. Thinking it might be a good time to swallow my pride, I caught his eye and asked for directions.

The only warmth I felt came from the hot sun overhead. We didn't seem to be making any human connection other than just discussing directions. I surely wasn't helping the situation with my self-focused attitude.

As we both were ready to proceed on our planned routes, I surprised myself by venturing, "Thanks. Once I was lost, but now I am found."

A wide smile broke out on his face, and the distance between us dissolved more quickly than a snowball would have melted on the broiling sidewalk. He pointed to his church, visible from where we were standing. "Same here, brother. Same here."

I don't remember if we hugged outwardly, but I know we did inside. The blight around me changed to character, and strangers became fellow sojourners. I felt as if I were glowing. People returned my smile as I worked my way back to the trail. Maybe *I* was the snarky one at the bus stop.

I think I was meant to hike alone, get lost, and take the trail I did that day so that my "found brother" could help me gain a fresh perspective. Not many situations in my life have more greatly affected the way I view those who don't live in my tiny world.

I recently went back to finish out this section with a two-day hike in the Cuyahoga Valley with Poppie-no-Stoppie and his friend Peggy. I hardly dared to believe I would find any more blessings than I had already been granted here. It soon became clear, though, that they hadn't ended yet.

Peggy, unable to hike due to knee problems, met us halfway through the first day with sandwiches and drinks on her tailgate. Poppie and I greedily consumed, among other goodies, slabs of turkey and ham. Peggy then drove off to that night's camp, having earned quite a few "angel points." They wouldn't be her last this trip.

Poppie had planned the hike well. He had made arrangements earlier for us to spend the night at a Cuyahoga National Park farm just off the trail. We were all grateful for such a hospitable place to stay.

We rounded up both of the vehicles, set up camp, and built a fire from the wood provided by Laura, the resident manager of the farm. Then Peggy performed more food magic when she summoned up ground beef, onions, potatoes, carrots, butter, and tinfoil. I almost needed a pinch to believe it. Was this for real?

The next day Peggy ran support vehicle again for Poppie and me. She also created one of the best trail magic moments for me so far. Poppie and I had wandered off the trail a mile or so. I think it was my fault, but I tried to wiggle out of the blame anyway. This time, though, nobody had to backtrack to the trail because Peggy came and got us. Another instance of an angel getting hikers back on track. Peggy had racked up countless more angel points.

After a visit to McDonald's at the end of the day, Peggy, Poppie, and I parted ways. I was tired but happy; I had finished the Akron section.

The following day Poppie e-mailed me a cell phone picture that had both shocked and pleased him. Tears of gratitude moistened my eyes when I saw it. By some "trick" of light refraction, an angel shape surrounded me on the trail. Coincidence? By then, I was more than willing to believe it just might be a real angel, and Poppie apparently was too.

I will always be thankful for the unexpected blessings that popped up along the entire Akron section. I think those blessings are always out there waiting for us. We just need to have our eyes open to see them when they come, and be willing to accept them.

As BONNIE AND I TRAVELED to West Virginia on Wednesday morning, many different emotions were trying to rise to the surface of my heart and mind. Guilt, however, would pull each one back under so *it* could be the center of my attention.

When we arrived, Guilt was making me feel responsible for what had happened to Dave's young assistant. Brian had reported for work on Tuesday morning, only to find Dave dead on his couch, a .357 Magnum round having passed through his brain. If I had stayed at Dave's, Tuesday for Brian might have been just a normal day of repairing computers.

I wasn't ready to talk to him, but I tried calling him anyway. His parents answered and told me that he was too shaken to talk. I apologized to them and asked them to pass my regrets on to Brian. They weren't upset with me like I thought they would be.

Guilt made me think I was accountable for all of Dave's concerns. Dave had let his affairs fall apart as his life did the same. I felt personally responsible that the house had not been repaired, just as if I had been the one who had neglected it. I also thought, being the oldest sibling, that I was expected to be the executor of his estate. I didn't even know what being executor meant. I immediately started making promises that I would not be able to keep, like assuring Betty, his ex-wife, that I would see to it that the estate was settled quickly, even though I knew in reality that it would take months, or possibly years.

Guilt is a shrewd devil. It made me feel almost as if I had pulled that trigger myself. Thus, I was wary of talking to Jay, worried that he would be angry with me. To be sure, he was in shock at the sudden and tragic loss of his friend, but instead of anger, he showed compassion toward me and tried to help me bear my burden. I look back now on our talks as being a substantial part of the barrier against the tsunami that was threatening to crash over me.

Bonnie and I did a lot of walking and talking and praying in the same park in Huntington in which Dave and I had ridden our bikes. During my worst times, I have taken my pain to the dearest woman in my life, and she suffers it out with me. Her "faith bubble" was deep and wide enough for her to grab my hand and pull me in. It was a place of sanity in the middle of an insane situation.

The following day was the one I had most dreaded. Funerals are hard enough, but I felt as if I would be on trial, having to explain to all the victims how sorry I was.

Dave's friends and customers did not seem angry with me, though. In fact, they consoled me. Several shared that they had seen something strange happening with Dave but had not expected this. Dave's girlfriend, Debbie, was extremely welcoming to me. Bonnie and I had figured we might attend a service someday for her and Dave—but not this kind.

It must have been extremely difficult for the preacher to prepare his message about a young man who had taken his life. I looked out over the crowd. Lloyd sat near the front. He is hard for me to read sometimes because he doesn't usually wear his heart on his sleeve. That day he was wearing an uncustomary look of shock. Beside him was my son Matt, who has always seemed wiser than his years to me. He and I would now share a new level of understanding, not one I wished for either of us; he had sat in a service similar to this for *his* brother. Our relatives from Dorset had teary looks, maybe trying to figure out how those ashes could possibly belong to the nephew and cousin who just months before had kept them all laughing well into the night. The preacher had a hard time getting through the service himself. He hadn't known Dave long, but I could tell it had been long enough for him to be emotionally affected by his passing.

When the service ended, I made my way outside, still feeling numb. A group of Dave's acquaintances to whom he owed money began telling me about their financial matters.

Guilt was not letting go. Since I was "responsible," I assured them that I would do whatever I could to rectify each situation. Lloyd overheard the conversation. He was concerned and tried to rescue me from making any more impromptu commitments in my weakened state of mind.

Bonnie and I traveled home with heavy hearts, but in a few days returned to face the monumental task before us. We knew nothing of settling estates, and Dave's involved not only his house, but also his business. Stacks of mail, both opened and unopened, were scattered throughout his office, containing, we supposed, numerous unpaid bills. There were the house repairs needing to be made. Betty, also assuming me to be the executor, expected me to take care of them.

Where to even begin. It would be difficult enough if I lived close; how was I to take care of things from 160 miles away? In front of us stood a mountain that we couldn't see a way over or around. There was more walking and praying in the park, followed by a sleepless night.

Things were no clearer when morning arrived. We still had absolutely no idea what to do. I decided to call one of Dave's friends about a legal question. After he answered my question, I shared with him the turmoil we were in. I soon found out that the decision to call him that morning was no accident.

From our conversation, I learned that I did not need to be executor of Dave's estate; I could assign the settlement of the estate to the county by simply signing a paper. In the instant of hearing that fact, the unmovable mountain disintegrated.

Bonnie and I stared at each other through the settling dust, unable to speak at first. We gradually realized that a huge answer to our prayers had just come. We quickly drove to the courthouse where I signed that paper, as well as another that would turn over to Betty anything I might have gotten from Dave's estate. The one thing I couldn't turn over to anyone else, though, was the debilitating work Guilt was doing on me.

Bonnie and I went back home that day, our burdens greatly lightened. But I would still have the emotional burden to deal with.

SINKING SPRING SECTION

Camping on BT property near Serpent Mound

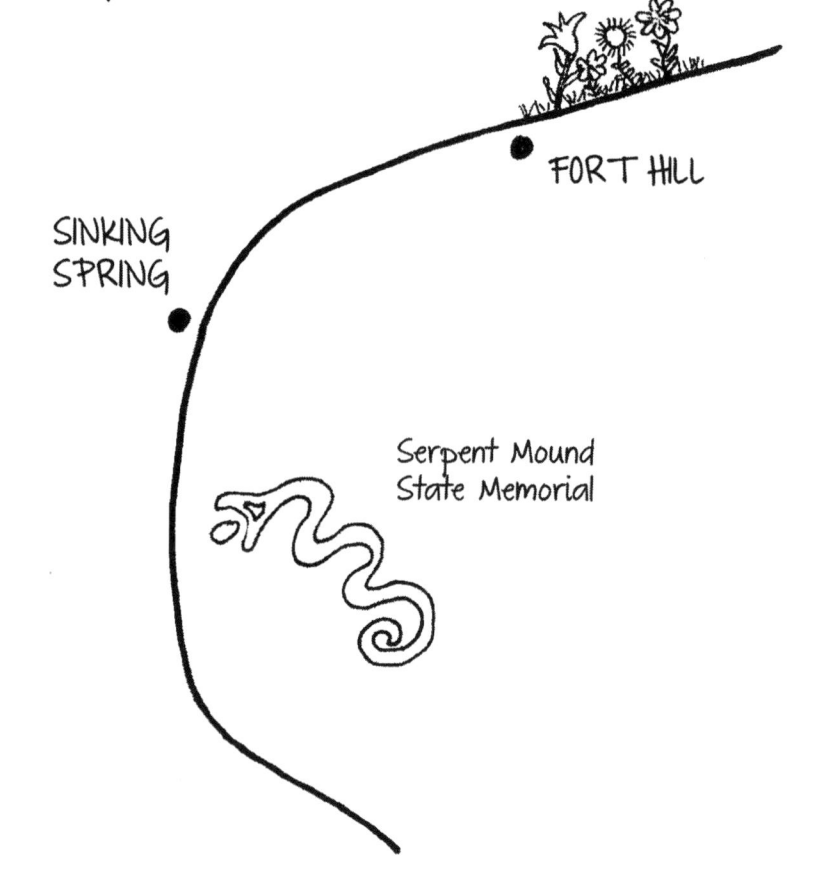

SINKING SPRING

● FORT HILL

Serpent Mound State Memorial

Journal Entry #23

Finding Clues

Several other guys and I followed the Buckeye Trail right into the park at Serpent Mound State Memorial. There were no crop circles like the ones reported a while back in the soybean field across from the entrance. Nor were there any glowing orange "earth lights." We didn't see any flying objects like the ones described on another occasion by deputies from Adams and other surrounding counties. Sorry to disappoint you. Nothing there but a 1,300-foot snake.

That area of the Sinking Spring section of the trail might have been like any other field, forest, or town in Adams County had it not been for the efforts of Frederick Ward Putnam of the Peabody Museum at Harvard in the late 1800s. He appreciated the Ohio mounds, so when he saw many of them being plowed or developed, he wanted to do something to preserve them. With the help of a group of women in Boston, he raised enough money for the museum to buy 60 acres for the snake to slither around in. As a result, we have Serpent Mound, the largest surviving example of a prehistoric effigy mound in the world.

The snake was there all right, coiled with open mouth. Perhaps it was about to swallow a bird or a rodent. Maybe even a human sacrifice. Luckily, about 200 yards separated our camp from the hungry-looking reptile.

Many questions exist concerning Serpent Mound, one of the biggest being who built it. The mound is three feet high and up to twenty feet wide. (It seems like a lot of work to me just digging a cat hole every morning when camping.) Some scholars give credit to the pre-Adenas, others to the Adenas, and still others to the Hopewell or Fort Ancient cultures. If the most recent dating work is accurate, the snake is slightly less than 1,000 years old. That would seem to indicate that the Fort Ancients were the builders.

However, as soon as the question seems to get answered, other information leads in a different direction. Even though the Fort Ancients fit the timeline for construction of the mound, historically they would have more likely created a rattlesnake. Also, they usually placed artifacts in their mounds, but this dirt-snake's belly appears to be empty. And the remains in the surrounding mounds are buried in a manner inconsistent with the Fort Ancient culture.

We came across other sticklers as well. The oval-to-head area points to the summer solstice sunset, while one of the coils may point to the winter solstice sunrise and another to the equinox sunrise. Where did the builders obtain all of this astronomical knowledge? Did the builders know the snake overlooks a huge crater? And what formed the crater? An asteroid, or maybe volcanic action?

As we pondered all of those questions, our attention shifted to a group of African-American witches who walked through our camp on their way to a nearby field. They had beautiful robes, long dreadlocks, and sparkly gold jewelry. If I recall correctly, they said they were descended from the earliest Native Americans. We talked briefly, but they were pressed to reach the field. That night they danced on the snake.

We ended our backpacking trip in Fort Hill, a major destination for hikers. The 33-acre area is worthy of that distinction. It has no shortage of spectacular scenery on its miles of trails, including gorges, old growth trees, and a ton of wildflowers.

It amazes me how lightly populated and heavily wooded this section of the BT is. It makes for some great hiking. For me, though, the Serpent Mound swallows most of my interest. And it reminds me that sometimes there are more questions than there are answers.

IN THE DAYS THAT FOLLOWED the funeral, I continued the conversation by phone with Dave's friends. I discovered that, to a person, they had noticed the changes going on in him and in his relationships in the last weeks and months. Before Dave completed suicide, they had sensed that he was making preparations for something, but they didn't know what. No one had deciphered the message that he was saying goodbye. Life's optometrist was now adjusting everybody's hindsight to 20-20.

It appeared as though Dave had said all his goodbyes in person since no one could find a note. I did find a story in his files that I thought could be considered a clue of sorts, but even then it wasn't clear. He wrote of faking a suicide, then confronting some people who sought to profit from it. It read like any of his other short stories.

Although the story may have been simply a product of his creative imagination, in retrospect, I realized that there were clues all along, clues as obvious as the pain in my heart. If they had been found and acknowledged just weeks or days before, they would have been called warning signs of a potential suicide. I discovered them everywhere my mind wandered:

- A huge bag of cat food torn open on the floor to give his cats unlimited access
- The laundry he did so he would be found in clean clothes
- The giant DQ burger that he enjoyed *one more time*
- The admonition that I need to get off the hamster wheel and step out there, as he gazed off in the distance
- His satisfaction at being able to witness the Phoenix Lander touch down safely *in his lifetime*
- The running up of his credit cards
- The drugs and alcohol
- The handgun for "self-defense"
- The goodbye hug
- *The paperback on my car seat*

I should have been able to see the signs. After all, guidance counselor is one of my certifications. I had even attended a workshop on suicide only three months earlier as part of my recertification process. Every classic sign I studied at that workshop was being displayed by Dave.

As his brother, was I un*able* to see the truth, or just un*willing* to see it?

MEDINA SECTION

A lonely back road on a dreary day

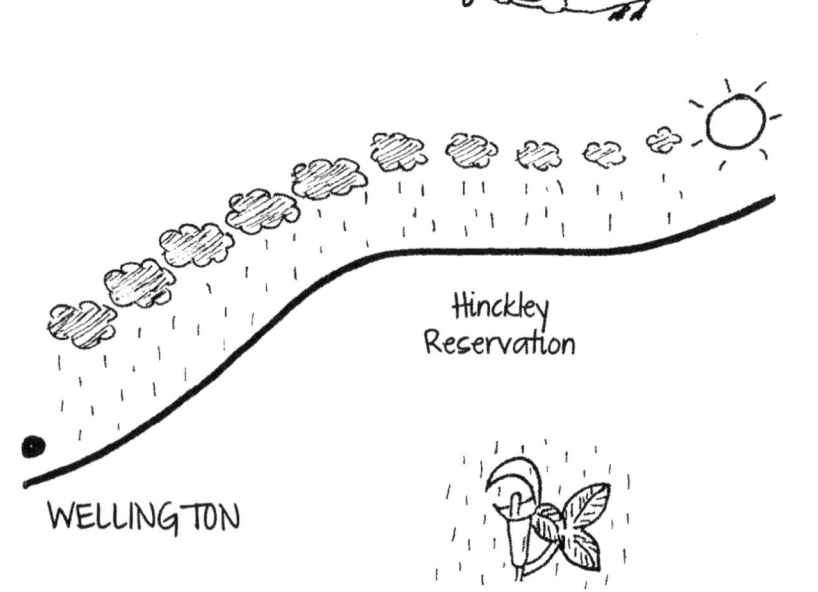

Hinckley Reservation

WELLINGTON

Journal Entry #24

Remembering the Big Picture

The rain was falling steadily on the chilly May morning as Bob and I began our 21.7-mile day in the Medina section. My plantar fasciitis was throbbing, worsened by a 60-mile hike just over a week before. I was not a happy hiker, but I broke out my umbrella and forged ahead anyway.

Not only was it a rainy day, but it was also a Monday. Both of those factors bring out my worst moods. It didn't help at all when we came across a litter of kittens abandoned and exposed to the weather. The rain had about done them in. Since we had no cell signal, Bob and I stopped at the next farm and asked the owner if he would call the SPCA. He said he would try, but he thought that they only came for dogs because they might form packs and become a nuisance. We would not know the outcome of the kittens' plight. The dreary day stretched out before us.

I listened to the rain ping on my minivan roof all that night. Despite my fervent wishing and best prayers, the rain didn't go away as the morning came around.

Bob and I drove to Subway in nearby Wellington for breakfast. They remembered us from our last big hike in the area, and once again we got royal treatment. That was good. I thought if we got warm, dry, and full, Bob might just say we should go home. Then I would offer a weak argument before reluctantly agreeing. If anything, though, Bob seemed invigorated by the hearty breakfast. *Rats!*

We parked the cars a little closer together that day so that we could try to dry out in them every few miles. The weather turned chillier and the rain came down harder. When we reached Hinckley Reservation, Bob excitedly pointed out a soaking wet jack-in-the-pulpit. I wasn't exactly in the mood to look at wildflowers.

Even when we crossed the highest point on the BT, 1,290 feet above sea level, I still felt low. We were not far from Buzzard Roost. Turkey vultures have returned there on the fifteenth of every March since 1957. Good thing they were not flying overhead that day as pitiful as I must have looked limping along.

At the end of the day we decided to splurge: we went to Cracker Barrel and then checked into a motel. We had about 16 miles to go the next day to finish up the section. I desperately hoped they would be warm and dry miles.

I was deeply disappointed the next morning when I peeked out the window and saw that the rain was still falling on the red roof. But then I remembered that it was the last day of the hike. I could make it one more day. I knew that my tunnel had an end and I would soon be spotting a glimmer of light.

I didn't even have to wait all day. By noon, soothing patches of blue began to appear over our heads. My limp had not lessened, but the pain wasn't quite as fierce.

I realize now, Dave, that for you there was no light. Not even a glimmer. You were not able to see past the pain and the dreary skies. This wasn't like a foot injury that could be fixed with time and therapy. In your mind, the problem was "you"—and you knew only one way to take care of it.

A FEW DAYS AFTER DAVE'S FUNERAL, I received a call from our cousin Donnie who had been enjoying his smoothly-running computer since Dave had fixed it the fall before. Donnie sounded as if he was shaken to the core. He said that the first time he turned his computer on after Memorial Day, he was greeted with the little ditty Dave had sung into the mic many months before. Apparently, Dave's plan had been in the works for quite some time.

Maybe, though, Dave had left his options open until Memorial Day, hoping for a miracle that would change his life. If that had occurred, we would have been laughing at that little tune. It could have eventually become a celebration song for having an article accepted by *National Geographic*, getting a story published, or realizing consistent profits in his computer business.

I am not angry with Dave. I understand that continued depression affects brain chemistry. That it can disable the brain—precisely the organ needed to "fix" oneself. He needed brain power to figure a way out of his mess, but he was powerless. Powerless to see the bigger picture.

I *am* angry that it happened. Dave could have become larger than life. He seemed to have all the raw material necessary. Now we will never know what might have been. Any chance of a great legacy is gone. And I will never know what new paths our relationship might have traveled.

I often wish I could forget that Memorial Day and everything associated with it. Forget the pain, the nightmares, the anger, the sadness. Occasionally I find myself wishing that I could get a redo, that I could go back in time and stay at Dave's house one more day rather than coming home. That little ditty might have turned into a victory song of my success at helping him. In a way, this is a long story about failure, of a missed opportunity.

However, after six years, I find that most of the time I accept reality and remember Dave's Life rather than his End. The hikes that brought us together after those years we drifted apart. His vivid imagination, which he so skillfully used to stretch mine. And his gentle spirit, which now that I look back on it, looks a lot like humility. Yes, that's the bigger picture of Dave. I can see it now.

PEMBERVILLE SECTION

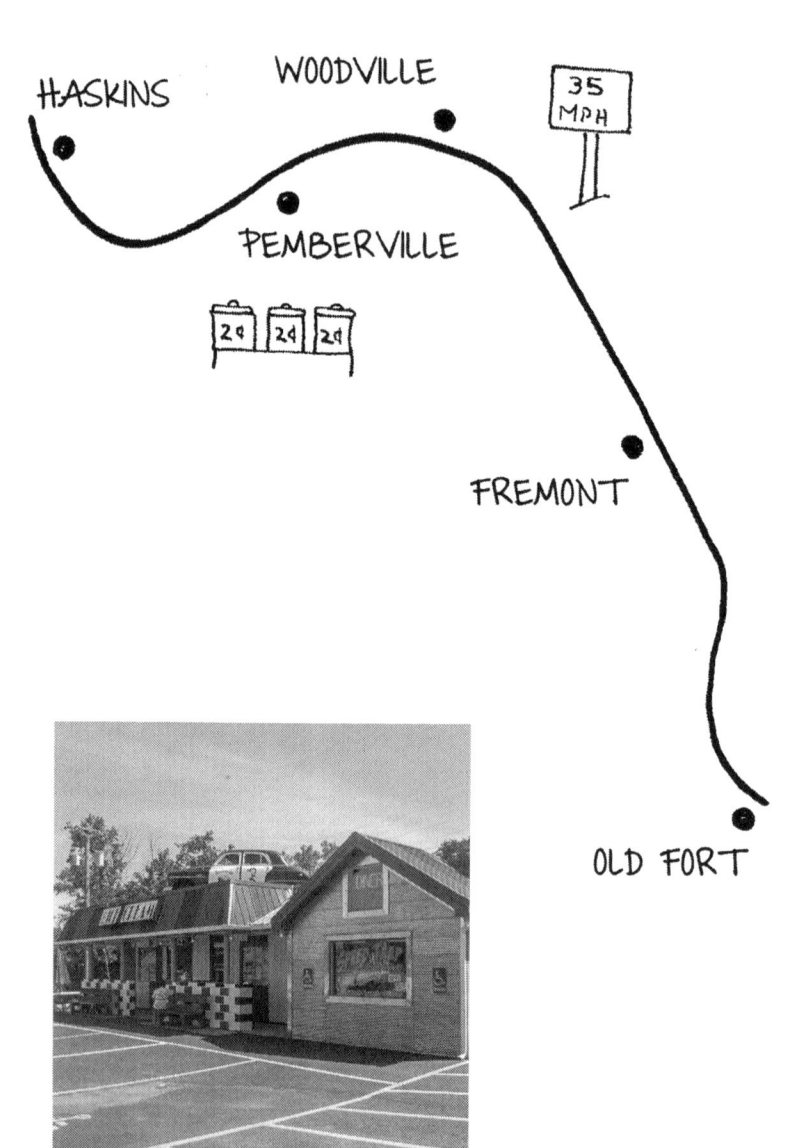

HASKINS

WOODVILLE

35 MPH

PEMBERVILLE

2¢ 2¢ 2¢

FREMONT

OLD FORT

Speed Trap Diner & Dairy
with a cherry on top

Journal Entry #25

Remembering the Good Ole Days

Not far into the Pemberville section, the realization that I was running out of miles hit me like the torrent of air from the last passing truck. State Route 64 became Memory Lane. As Bob and I hiked past soybeans, corn, wheat, and other bounty rising up from the rich farmland, we began swapping stories gleaned from a rich crop of shared miles and experiences on the Buckeye Trail.

Bob confessed, "I didn't think I would be hiking 750 miles with someone packing an exploding olive oil bottle."

To that I replied, "Let's keep our facts straight. It was an exploding *cold-pressed, extra virgin* olive oil bottle."

To be sure, we had reminisced quite a bit on earlier hikes, but this one was special. This section was our last one as a team, at least until after I finish the BT. I do have one more section to complete, but Bob will be needed in Florida soon to begin the proper spoiling of his new grandchild.

We entered the small village of Haskins still in our nostalgic mood and working up a thirst. Getting a drink in this town a century ago was dangerous for one man. An altercation at the saloon led to his fatal stabbing at the town pump. I, however, found refreshment safely at the corner grocery store.

"What do you think was our most dangerous exploit on our hikes?" I asked Bob as the silhouette of the town faded behind us.

"You mean besides discussing politics when we should have been watching for blazes?"

Bob had a point. The six most dreaded words on the trail might be, "Have you seen a blaze lately?"

We pondered on that one until I revived the conversation. "I have to go with the guy on the ATV who told us to ignore the blaze right in front of us because it shouldn't be there. That was a new one."

"Yeah, that's when I was thinking that *we* shouldn't have been there."

"How about that pack of 'coyotes' that stalked us?"

"That was almost as bad as when I slid my car to the edge of that cliff."

All of those incidents had taken place on the Wilderness Loop, and it was a surprise to neither of us that our memories took us there. Sure, it was the source of many difficulties. However, if we had it to do all over again, I don't think either of us would change a thing.

When we reached our car in Pemberville on day two, we skipped that burg temporarily, hurried on to Woodville, and pulled cautiously into the speed trap for which the village is noted—Speed Trap Diner & Dairy, that is. You would have loved it, Dave. There was a '50-something, black-and-white cherry top cruiser sitting atop the building. Inside the diner we became lost in the '50s and '60s. I expected to see the Fonz walk in, thump the jukebox, and head to the restroom to check out his hair. We definitely planned to check out that place again.

Bob had to go home after we ate. I walked back to Pemberville, alone with my thoughts. What was I going to do after I finished the BT? I realized that hiking was habit-forming and that I would be working up another major hike, God willing. In fact, I was already giving serious thought to a thru-hike of the BT. I might be disappointed, though, try-

ing to recapture the great memories of this three-year journey on a rehike. The second time around, I might not
- Win the battle with the "trail dog"
- Catch a ride in a monster truck
- Meet cross-country hikers as personable as Karen and Jerry
- Receive tableside service at Subway
- Get pulled over by policemen as professional as the ones in Huron County
- Encounter my very own angel in the Akron section
- Find such a great bunch of new friends to share the experience with

I tucked these thoughts away as I reached Beeker's General Store. Inside, I was greeted with a row of two-penny candy in huge glass jars. At least that's what first grabbed my attention. Other goodies and crafts lined the shelves, and I could almost picture people coming in to "grocery and gossip" back in the day. I didn't involve myself in gossip, but I did purchase a big glass jug of blueberry cider and some delicious spaghetti pretzels. The owner, Todd, helped me record my visit by snapping my photo out front just before I headed back to Kentucky.

Bob and I returned a couple of weeks later to finish the section. Of course we had to start where we left off the last time: the Speed Trap. This time the cruiser perched on the roof had company. A modern police vehicle sat idling out front.

If I was going to be picked up for speeding, I would want it to be by the policeman in that cruiser (the one on the ground). We spent at least ten minutes chit-chatting with him through the cruiser window, having found still another just plain friendly guy along the trail. No wonder they have a burger named after him. We did notice, however, that he kept one eye on speeds popping up on his dash as daring motorists ventured through *his* speed trap.

Back inside, Bob enjoyed a burger again this visit; I scarfed a huge omelet. Not that we had to hurry. We had only 26 miles to do in two days, and on this flat terrain, it would basically be a stroll.

We headed east. The sun was hot, but we enjoyed a breeze and low humidity. We hopped on a rail trail in Elmore to make the trip to Fremont. No train now, just a walking trail. We would be taking the "sole train." (Sorry, Dave. I couldn't help myself.)

That part of the BT had just been rerouted onto the North Coast Inland Trail, a bikeway slated to eventually link Toledo to Cleveland and Akron. I savored the stretch we were on that day. It was quiet and calm, allowing us the freedom to talk again about the good ole days. We just needed to keep a watch out for the occasional passing bike.

Bob got the conversation back on track. "What are you going to do next?"

"I'm not sure, but life is not going to be the same again until I'm covered with ticks and poison ivy, lost without a blaze in sight, and bogged down in a mucky horse trail with a dog on my tail."

"I hear *that*."

After camping at the Travel Lodge in Fremont, we hiked the next day to Old Fort. The trail basically followed the Sandusky River. Bob had his car parked—with permission this time—at a huge warehouse. The building was full of cannons, bells, and many other props for use in such things as movies and documentaries.

I wonder if they ever supply items to reality shows.

Remembering the Good Ole Days

I STILL HAVE THE IMPULSE to call Dave when anything exciting happens. Tonight was exciting! The final American Idol show of the season was on TV.

Bonnie and I enthusiastically traded opinions as to the crown-ability of the two finalists. I texted a buddy of mine to get his valued opinion. I listened to the judges' take. However effective all of this was in reducing my pre-show jitters, though, something was still missing this evening. I still wanted to call Dave for the "official" prediction.

After the winner was finally named and then dug out from under the deluge of confetti, the urge to call Dave hit again—even after years of stifling it. I wanted Dave's post-show analysis, his glowing endorsement or maybe some of his sarcastic comments.

Years ago Dave invited me to Wayne County to watch his new big screen TV with him. We brewed up a huge pot of coffee and set up the snack buffet on the coffee table. We adjusted the comfy new viewing chairs to the perfect angle. Satisfied that all preliminaries had been covered, Dave ceremoniously grasped the remote and hit the power button.

I was amazed at the realism. So was Dave, even though he had already been enjoying his new toy for days. We were live at Season 4 of American Idol!

Bo and Constantine were still vying for the rocker crown, and we were prepared to sing along. We tried to guess what they would belt out this time. I don't recall what Bo sang that night—no offense to Bo—but I'll never forget Constantine's selection.

When the dark silhouette of the contestant appeared, we grabbed our air guitars and readied ourselves to rock. Electrifying anticipation, though, suddenly gave way to dissonance between our fingers and our brains. Was that "Ba ba ba ba ba ba ba ba ba ba ba ba ba?" Yes, it was "I Think I Love You" by The Partridge Family with David Cassidy!

Our immediate reaction was to look at each other in disbelief. Constantine's song choice was totally unexpected. Who knew the Partridge Family was a rock group? But then grins slowly widened across our faces, and we fingered our guitars again. We rocked right along with Constantine. In the following weeks, we exchanged many calls to express our mutual admiration for our new favorite rock song and singer.

Besides our shared interest in American Idol, another bittersweet memory stems from a call I made to Dave a few years later, this time from Sam's Club. I had found an awesome backpack and wanted to know if he was interested in it. He was, so I bought it for him and took it on my next visit. He acted as if it was a treasure to rival his prized big screen TV.

The pack was divided into two roomy compartments in the main sack, as well as two small ones in the top flap. It was equipped with countless loops, belts and straps, besides having a plethora of pouches in all sizes—even tiny ones on the hip belt. Some pouches were made of black webbing, some had zippers, and a large inside pouch was insulated to carry a camel of cold water, or perhaps some warm soup.

This was a massive upgrade from what we had used on the AT. Dave sat staring at that bag, wide-eyed at the prospects of what would go where. No more dumping everything into the big open tube of his other sack. Now he could find bear food or bear spray at a moment's notice. We would be ready when it came time for the Big Trip.

Too bad we weren't styling with Sam's backpacks years ago when we proudly hiked with Eight Bear and Kitchen Sink. And when it came to Caveman, we would have known exactly where to find whatever he was bumming. We could have used them to pack our stuff for our trips to Canada and secretly laughed while we watched the border agents search through the endless compartments for contraband.

I don't know where Dave's backpack ended up. I haven't been back to Wayne County since 2008. At that time I requested his pack, but I never heard anything more about it. Maybe it has found its way onto the back of someone hiking the AT. If so, I would want him to know that Dave probably had some sweets tucked away in the handy hip-belt pouch, concealing them from me or any Cavemen out there.

TROY SECTION

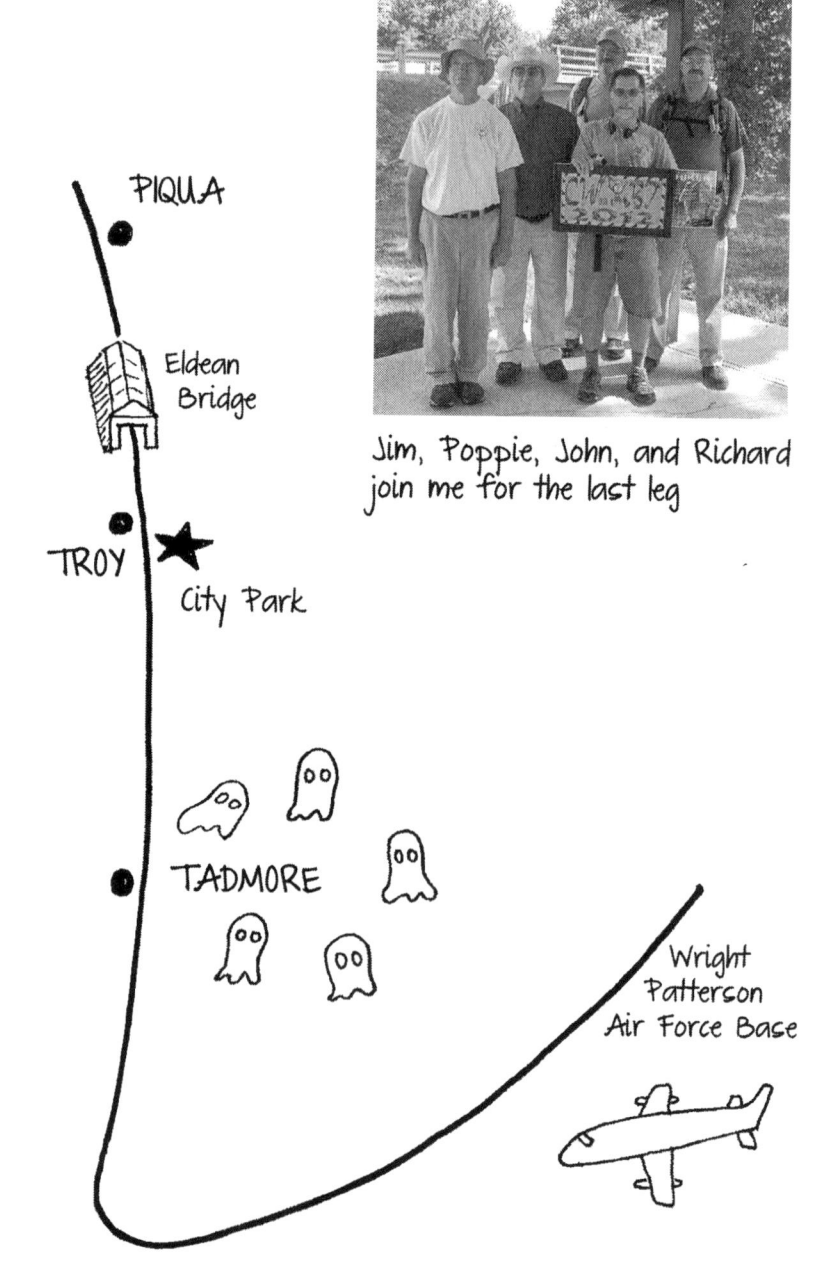

Jim, Poppie, John, and Richard join me for the last leg

- PIQUA
- Eldean Bridge
- TROY ★ City Park
- TADMORE
- Wright Patterson Air Force Base

Journal Entry #26

Remembering a Son

Even though I hiked most of the miles in the Troy section early in my BT journey, I planned from the beginning to complete my hike in the city of Troy. I wanted to end up at your nephew and my son's resting place.

I began this section way back in 2009 when I hiked the seven miles north of Piqua with Charles. We heard about a working canal boat at Johnston Farm & Indian Agency in the area, but our one-day trip didn't allow us enough time to enjoy a ride on it.

A couple of months later, I hiked ten miles with Jim. We walked through a stretch of woods along a chain link fence that separated us from Wright Patterson Air Force Base. The National Museum of the U.S. Air Force is located there. I'd visited it many times before. I am amazed at the numbers of aircraft displayed at the museum and that everything there is free to view.

The following month I hiked fourteen miles alone. The trail took me through a ghost town called Tadmore. The ghosts were quiet that day. However, in the mid-nineteenth century, it must have been anything but serene. It was a busy crossing for traffic on the Old National Road (Route 40), keelboats on the Great Miami River, canal boats in the Miami-Erie Canal, and trains on the Dayton-Michigan Railroad. Eventually, river traffic gave way to the canal boats; then the canal was replaced by the railroad. Later, flooding caused the National Road to be rerouted. The few residents of Tadmore eventually decided it was time to leave.

At the end of that year, Bonnie and I hiked on a brisk December day. She hates cold weather, so I knew that she didn't appreciate the fashion statement the icicles on her hat made. I thought she looked great, out of her element, out *in* the elements. The icicles had formed over a period of hours. We hiked more than twelve miles northward to Troy from the spot where her dad had dropped us off.

Some of those miles were on busy highways. Although my map said we were on the trail, part of the way we saw only faint gray marks where the blazes should have been. Bonnie insisted they must be badly faded blazes since they were the exact size and shape for BT markers. We had no choice but to follow them.

When I checked the map updates on the BT website the next day (which I should have done *before* the hike), I discovered that the trail had been rerouted to the much quieter and more hiker-friendly bike trail. The gray paint was intended to hide the blue blazes. It didn't hide them well enough for us, but that was good because it gave us something to follow, even if it was the old route.

Close to our destination that day, we passed beneath the trestle in Troy. I was glad Bonnie was there to support me. Once again, she was there when I needed her, and I whispered a prayer of thanks.

On that cold, dismal afternoon, I thought of how Mark's passing must have had a significant effect on you. The two of you were so much alike. You must have had an idea of how he felt as he walked down those tracks for the last time.

We had shuttled our car that morning to City Park, which was located across the road from the cemetery. We knew we would be returning to the park from the opposite direction someday. The hike that day left me with less than nine miles to finish the Troy section, miles reserved for those final steps of my multiyear trek.

□ □ □

THE FINAL MILES—With the recent completion of all but the last eight and a half miles of the BT, it was now time to finish my quest. I arranged for it to take place during the two-week visit of Bonnie's brother and sister-in-law. Mike and Rosy would be coming from their home in Costa Rica and were eager to participate in the finale.

Since some non-hikers would be joining me for the last stretch, I decided to have mercy on them and shorten it. A week before my planned finishing date, Bonnie and I hiked six of the remaining miles. We started at Eldean Bridge, built over the Great Miami in 1860. It is the longest "Long Truss" covered bridge in the nation. I was surprised the first time I saw a car pop out of it, even though it looks more than solid enough to drive across.

We hiked north towards Piqua, mostly on the bike trail. The plan was for Mike, Rosy, and Bonnie's dad to meet us in Piqua. In order to synchronize our arrival times, Bonnie kept in touch with Mike by texting, so much so that it seemed as though he was walking with us. Since she finds it difficult to text and walk at the same time, I was provided with ample chances to catch up to her.

On the way to our destination, we passed the first atomic power plant in the country. I could hardly believe it was right there on the bike trail. Even though it is no longer operable, I was energized just to walk past such a structure. We met the family at the Lighthouse Restaurant where we enjoyed friendly service and home cooking before making our way home.

Twenty-four hours before the final day, it looked to be a washout. Bonnie was dismayed when she heard the same weather report for the third time that day. It was still guaranteeing just short of a flood.

"It's OK," I encouraged her. "Hikers are used to rain."

"Well, I'm not a hiker," she replied without missing a step.

No problem, though. Wednesday arrived and the sky was clear. Bonnie's dad dropped Mike, Rosy, and us off at Eldean Bridge. Waiting for us there were John and Jane, friends who live in Troy. Their schedule didn't allow them to hike, but they wanted to stop by to offer congratulations. Hiking buddies, Poppie, Richard, Jim, and John were also gathered there. John had brought three of his grandkids.

Greetings were exchanged. Photos were taken. Gifts were received. Poppie had made a framed remembrance of my BT hike and had also created a magazine cover proclaiming my accomplishment. Jim gave me some great photos he had taken of our hikes together. My anticipation was high as I took my first steps toward the bridge.

Shortly after we set out, Dad passed our already-stretched-out group as he drove the two and a half miles to City Park in Troy to await our arrival. Charles was running late and would meet us at the park as well.

Between conversations, I found time for some personal reflection on my BT journey.

This hike wasn't about ticking off miles, though there were a few days where it seemed as if that was exactly what it was all about. Rather, it was about reaching milestones, from surviving that first eye-opening backpacking trip to conquering the challenging Wilderness Loop to finally completing the entire BT.

It was about walking through history. In this section alone I saw working canal boats, a national museum, a ghost town, an atomic power plant, and a record-setting covered bridge. Multiply that by the 26 sections of the Buckeye Trail, and I've taken an Ohio history course. I'll retain this a lot better than the course I took in eighth grade.

I found more than history along the trail. I found my inner child joining me on the loop, urging me to enjoy the experience and not to be so serious. I found a willingness to laugh at my insecurities and trust the Lord a little more. I found drama and adventure that you would have reveled in.

I found that my family cared enough about me to stick with me, watch my slide shows, and at least look like they were listening to my often repeated tales. I found new hiking friends—no, I consider them brothers—five of whom were with me that day. They knew why I was there, they showed up, and they walked those last miles beside me. I found the reason that Captain Blue, who did complete his thru-hike in 2011, is still raving about it. It's true that the people and places on the trail make it more than worth the effort to follow the blue blazes around Ohio.

I lost some things as well (besides my cellphone). Just as I learned that there are some things I don't need to stuff into my backpack, there are feelings of despair and guilt I don't need to carry inside me. They are heavy and weigh me down, preventing me from moving forward. And they take up way too much room. They crowd out more important things like healing and laughter and new experiences—and the good memories.

I did a lot of remembering on this journey. Much of it was of all the adventures you and I shared at Red River Gorge, the Shawnee Day Hike Trail, the Greenbrier River Trail, the AT, and Cranberry River. So many childhood memories also came back to me, perhaps in a different light now since I can no longer hash them over with you. I remembered with fondness how you always looked up to your older brother, and I hope that is the way you felt when we parted. Parting well is important to me.

In spite of all my wandering thoughts, the last miles went quickly and I found myself near the end of my journey. We walked past the cemetery where Mark, whom I love with all my heart, was laid to rest in 2003. Bonnie's dad joined us on the levy along City Park with his dog Sugar, who is now officially a trail dog, for the homestretch. Few things compare to reaching a major goal surrounded by those who are dear to you. People who helped make it happen, sometimes by simply walking beside you.

I made it, Dave. I survived the trail, and yes, the trials. It wasn't the adventure we had planned together. You couldn't be there walking beside me the way I wanted, but you were definitely in my heart—every step of the way. I wish I could leave this journal on your car seat. I guess I'll have to wait a bit to tell you about it.

AT MARK'S PASSING, he was exactly half Dave's age, but even as I picture them both in my mind today, I sometimes have to think twice in order to separate them into two individuals. They were alike in so many ways. Both of them were intelligent, compassionate, and sensitive. They had strong beliefs. And they admired and loved each other.

When I think of those two, I inevitably return to Indian River Lodge on Rice Lake in Ontario. Dave, Mark, and I are lazing across our seats in the rowboat, lines in the water, but the fish don't seem to have an appetite for the menu we offer. The only thing bobbing is the boat. The warm breeze blowing over us brings mellow fishy smells that reward our olfactory nerves, totally worth the 800-mile drive.

The boom box is playing Dave's favorite Bach cassette, loud enough for the fish to hear for many meters. Mark kids him about being an egghead. In my opinion, they both fit into that category. When Mark is able to pirate the player, he loads in some Christian rock by Petra, his favorite group. Dave complains about Mark's "angry music." Dave and Mark were both angry at times: angry at injustice, angry at hypocrisy. Sometimes they seemed to absorb all the pain in the world.

Like Dave, Mark was a sensitive soul, maybe the most sensitive person I will ever know. When he lost his sister Jami, she took a part of him with her. She was ten, he was eight, and a lot of his life experiences were attached to her. His older brother Matt was thirteen at the time, and despite the pain, I saw Matt nurture him as they struggled together into their sisterless future.

Dave and Mark were both youngest siblings, set apart by personality as well as birth-order. They were definitely less inhibited than their brothers and sisters and were not afraid to occasionally rock the boat. Both were also strong-willed. They required more explanation than "because I'm your father."

Mark shared Dave's love of nature. In fact, he was so fond of it that when he was six years old he came into the house one day with a large cicada stuffed into each ear. I carefully grabbed the legs of the critters and was greatly relieved when I was able to pull each insect out in one piece. Considering all the eardrops, tubes, and antibiotics it took to keep his ears healthy, he didn't need any help getting them infected. I asked him why he had stuffed them in and he answered, "I like listening to them." I should have known the answer before I asked. As Mark entered his later teen years, he gave up fishing to protect the fish, and in his early twenties he gave up his car and rode a bike everywhere to save the environment.

Mark drifted into the drug scene, and my admonitions to him only seemed to drive him in deeper. In 2003, I was excited when he entered treatment. However, I still had concerns about him because he was involved in a relationship that could never fly.

One day in the summer of that year, I picked Mark up in Troy and brought him to Kentucky for a visit with Bonnie and me. He was clean cut and his color was good. His smile was bright and he looked happy again. In fact, he looked like the picture of health.

We ate pizza on the porch. Then he played his guitar and sang, mostly songs he had written. Mark had been through a lot in his short life and wanted to talk about things. He seemed satisfied just to have two pairs of listening ears. Later he wanted to watch old episodes of "Little House on the Prairie" like we used to. I conked out early as usual, but he and Bonnie watched more episodes and talked well into the morning.

The next day the time seemed to fly as we all talked and laughed. Things were looking good. I was not ready for goodbye, but I needed to get Mark back to Troy.

A couple of months later, I was washing my car when the phone rang. It was Mark's mother. She told me that Mark had been hit by a CSX train on the trestle over the Great Miami River in Troy. Somehow, even as my brain was going into shock, I was able to keep listening as she relayed the details. He had reported to his workplace on his day off, distressed at having lost his phone. Not finding it there, he stopped by the house of the lady who didn't share his romantic interests. After leaving her place, he chose to cross the trestle, only succeeding partway.

The police report called it an apparent suicide. Matt did not think it was. If anyone should know it should be family. Right? You'd think. Mark's Bible study leader turned over to the police a note written by Mark that she found on a church bulletin. Mark sounded hopeless and helpless. It was a note that could have been taken different ways. The detective took it as a suicide note.

As I sit in McDonald's writing this, I realize that the grieving process for Mark, which has been stuck in neutral for almost a decade, is starting to move forward again. Some things a father's mind is not hardwired for. One is the passing of his son. But I'm finding that in order to grieve for Dave, I must allow myself to feel the pain of missing Mark.

Healing can be found this side of Heaven, along with countless good memories to enjoy and laugh about. And it helps to know that I'll see Dave and Mark again.

I hope Heaven has rowboats. Maybe the boat from which Jesus calmed the storm is docked there on the shore of the Sea of Forgetfulness. Dave will have his Bach, and Mark will have his Petra music—sounding perhaps a little less angry.

And me? Maybe I'll be singing, "I think I love you. Isn't that what life is made of?"

Final Journal Entry

Bonnie and I were talking about you today, Dave, as we have so many times over the past six years since you left us. She brought up something that you might have found intriguing. I know I do. It's that I *have* "stepped out there," just like you encouraged me to do.

I guess you know that it bugged me when you said I should step out. Maybe I was defensive because I thought you were dissing my worldview, or maybe it was because, as the senior sibling, I was more used to dishing out advice than getting it. These past years, while I kept trying to figure out what in the world you were talking about, I was actually out in the world doing it.

I stepped out of my predictable life onto an unknown trail. I made some great new friends whom I would never have crossed paths with otherwise and encountered incredible experiences that I had thought were just for other people. I even managed to swallow quite a bit of my pride and admit my mistakes, leading me to write about my journey. Now, not only have we shared the love of reading a good book (however relative "good" is), but we also share the appetite for putting words to paper. Just one more way this journey has brought me closer to you.

You probably knew I would pout for a while, stew a little, but then eventually do it. Actually, stepping out was the only way I could go. Now I'm moving forward.

And I'll keep going—one step at a time—until I get there.

AFTERWORD

I have a good friend who is a survivor of his dad's suicide. Jon suffers from depression, just as his father did. He shared with me in an after-church conversation one day that he had signed a pledge—a pledge in which he promised *not* to follow in his father's final footsteps.

Being a soul with a predisposition to the blues myself, I know how easy it is to entertain a thought of calling it quits. I remember the first time that I did. As repulsive as the thought was, it did bring a small measure of comfort. The thought came easier the second time, and even easier the third.

But If I have learned anything from the experiences shared with you in this story, it is that I need to send that thought packing if it returns, whenever, wherever, and however it expresses itself. If I am tempted to let it set up camp, I'll swallow my pride and get help. Like Jon, I make a pledge, here and now.

Over the last decades, studies have been done to examine the question of whether or not a person gradually returns to his previous level of contentment after experiencing significant positive or negative events in his life. Tough times have temporarily paralyzed me, but I've always returned to my normal level. I've seen, though, that time does not always heal, as in my brother's case, so it's a good idea to have trusted friends and family members as part of a safety net.

I have also learned something about intervention. Now I take seriously *any* talk of suicide, even if the person claims to be joking or if, like my brother, he insists he wouldn't really do anything to hurt himself though every possible sign is evident. I need to react. Maybe even overreact. What would I have lost if I had done so with Dave?

If I can't get through to a person whom I perceive to be in danger, I need to ask someone to help me intervene. Now I know not to leave the person alone. I figure I can apologize later for meddling, but I may not have the opportunity to apologize for not meddling.

The sad fact is that suicides happen 80 times a day in the United States. Many of the people who knew I was writing this book are themselves suicide survivors, those who have lost loved ones to suicide. That group includes several of the guys I hike with. One of my hiking friends even completed suicide himself.

I have encountered this tragedy twice in my family, and I pray never again. Although the effects have somewhat faded, I don't expect them to ever totally disappear. But that's OK. Dave's and Mark's lives are constant reminders for me to reach out to others with the message of hope that I have received—hope for light for the person living in darkness, hope for wisdom for his loved ones to recognize warning signs and respond effectively, and hope for healing for the suicide survivor.

ACKNOWLEDGMENTS

This story was made possible courtesy of my loving wife Bonnie, the official translator of my garbled ramblings. With her as editor, co-designer of the maps, and everything else it takes to publish a book, I was in the best hands possible. She methodically rounded every learning curve to gain proficiency in each skill. When I do a project, I just want it done. When Bonnie takes on a project, she won't rest until it is done right.

Even more importantly, with her as helpmate I got through those first weeks and months of losing my son and then my brother, and she encouraged me to tell this story about them.

Thanks to Paula for the heart-to-heart conversations about our brother. Every time we talk about Dave, he seems a little closer.

Thanks to Dave's good friend Jay who was a friend to Bonnie and me during those darkest of days.

Thanks to Bonnie's brother Mike who read my very earliest writings of the book, and still he encouraged me to keep writing. The slick website he built provides a great place for me to practice writing about hiking and daily life and a place to show off my hiking photos. As the cover designer of this book, he was not happy until he sent us back twice to that site in Hocking Hills for more retakes of the cover photo, and I'm glad he did.

Thanks to fellow hiker Chris for giving me feedback on some of the early chapters of the book.

Thanks to critical readers Jim, Jon, Mike, Andrew, and Debbie whose feedback was invaluable. I need all the help I can get!

Thanks to Bob Pond for sharing *Follow the Blue Blazes* with the world. I used it quite often to enrich my experience on my circuit hike, and at least a time or two in writing *Hiking Without Dave*.

Thanks to Sam for help on the history of the Delphos section.

Thanks to Bob for putting up with me for over half of the trail. We are living proof that a Beaver and a Retriever make a great team. Quite often that combination gets itself involved in some memorable adventures.

Thanks to Jim who helped me (and other hikers) complete the trail while postponing his own finishing hike. I am thankful Bonnie and I were able to be with him when he finally finished the BT.

Thanks to Bruce—Poppie-No-Stoppie—for organizing all of those hikes. He was the Mormon half of a Baptist-Mormon hiking team, a team that loved each other like The Good Book says to. He passed last year, but I'll see him again on the trail in Heaven.

Thanks to Charles for reasoning with that farmer. And to Richard for helping me finish the Whipple section on that long weekend.

There were other people with whom I shared a path or two: Andy, Pat, Dave, Peggy and Jacob, Kathy, Liz, Diane, Dale, Darryl, Dori, Bob L., Craig, Brian, Michelle, and Harold (who has since passed). I think Harold taught me more about backpacking on my first hike on the BT than I learned on all the other hikes combined.

Thanks to John for organizing all those MAC hikes, and for refusing to take gas money for all the extra shuttling he did for me. And to my trail angels Jay, Dana and Lisa, Peggy,

Laura, Byron and Shannon, Jamie, and last, but not least, the man in Akron who helped this hopelessly lost hiker be found!

Thanks to all the volunteers who keep the BT open and improving.

I should also mention those folks at the Newport McDonald's who supplied endless cups of coffee while I worked on this book.

I probably forgot some really important person. It was not intentional. It's probably due to the gradual loss of brain cells that comes with age.

One more thing: Thanks to Jesus for being out there on the trail with me. There is *nowhere* I want to go without Him.

NOTES

Preface
Pond, Robert J. *Follow the Blue Blazes: A Guide to Hiking Ohio's Buckeye Trail.* Athens: Ohio UP, 2003. Print.
[Second edition released October 15, 2014:
Pond, Connie, and Robert J. Pond. *Follow the Blue Blazes: A Guide to Hiking Ohio's Buckeye Trail.* Second ed. Athens: Ohio UP, 2014. 276. Print.]
Merrill, John N. *A Walk in Ohio.* Derbyshire, England: Walk and Write, 2000. Print.

Chapter 2
"Belle Valley Section" Buckeye Trail map. Pt. 17. Worthington, Ohio: Buckeye Trail Association, Inc., 2005. Print.

Chapter 3
"ADT in Ohio/Kentucky." *American Discovery Trail: Ohio.* Web. 21 Oct. 2014.

Chapter 4
"Ohio.gov / Search." *Little Miami State Park.* Web. 21 Oct. 2014.

Chapter 5
"Shelby County Historical Society - Canals - Lockington." *Shelby County Historical Society - Canals - Lockington.* Web. 21 Oct. 2014.

Chapter 6
Christie, John Aldrich. *Thoreau as World Traveler.* New York: Columbia UP with the Cooperation of the American Geographical Society, 1965. Print.
Nash, Roderick. *Wilderness and the American Mind.* 3rd ed. New Haven, Conn.: Yale UP, 1982. Print.

Chapter 11
Smalley, Gary, and John T. Trent. *The Two Sides of Love*. Carol Stream, Ill.: Tyndale House, 1990. Print.

Chapter 14
Pond, Robert J. *Follow the Blue Blazes: A Guide to Hiking Ohio's Buckeye Trail*. Athens: Ohio UP, 2003. Print.

Chapter 16
"South Chagrin Reservation." *Cleveland Metroparks*. Web. 21 Oct. 2014.

"Kirtland Temple History." *Kirtland Temple History*. Web. 21 Oct. 2014.

Chapter 19
"Raccoon." *Wikipedia*. Wikimedia Foundation, 19 Oct. 2014. Web. 21 Oct. 2014.

"The Challenge of Old Man's Cave." *North Coast Muse*. Web. 21 Oct. 2014.

Chapter 21
Pond, Robert J. *Follow the Blue Blazes: A Guide to Hiking Ohio's Buckeye Trail*. Athens: Ohio UP, 2003. Print.

Chapter 23
"The Great Serpent Mound of Southern Ohio." *The Great Serpent Mound of Southern Ohio*. Web. 21 Oct. 2014.

"The Mystery of the Ancient Earthworks - What Is Serpent Mound?" *The Mystery of the Ancient Earthworks - What Is Serpent Mound?* Web. 21 Oct. 2014.

Chapter 24
"What's the Deal with the Return of the Buzzards in Hinckley Ohio?" *About*. Web. 21 Oct. 2014.

BUCKEYE TRAIL MAP

To follow my blog
or to view photos from my hikes on the
Buckeye Trail and other trails
visit my website:

http://cwspencer.com/

Contact me at:

cw@cwspencer.com

Made in the USA
Charleston, SC
29 November 2014